advance praise for

YOU DON'T HAVE TO DIE
TO GET TO HEAVEN

Sue Pearson's book eloquently weaves her meaningful experiences into an exquisitely beautiful tapestry, sharing life's heartaches, healing epiphanies, and profound forgiveness. As readers journey alongside Sue through these deeply touching stories, they too are transformed. Now, the world can also be inspired by the wisdom and love contained within these pages. ~ **DEBRA ANN KAISER**, IANDS Group Coordinator, Facilitator

Sue Pearson brings a message of hope that shows how our closest and often most conflicted relationships can be healed even after death. Her book is a thought-provoking exploration of 'miraculous forgiveness' that can help free us from wounds we carry and offers a glimpse of a radiant love that is always present. This book is delightful and talks about experiences that everyone can relate to. It made me feel like I was in one of those' thin places' where the Celts say the veil between heaven and earth is blurred. ~ **THE REV. DEBRA SABINO**, Church of Our Savior

I am captivated by this series of "lifestories". Sue's narrative is woven with stories of what could be considered tragedy, tales of the ordinary, and re-telling of the truly extraordinary. The threads that permeate are ones of resilience, grace, and a resounding gratitude for all of life's gifts. I am reminded again of what keeps me committed to my 30-year career as a hospice social worker and bereavement counselor — the hope that can be found after tremendous loss, and the possibility of finding deep meaning and a connection to the Divine." ~ **CHRISTINE KOVACH, LCSW**

Sue Pearson takes us on an empowering spiritual journey through her life stories. We gain a better understanding of who we really are through the lens of love or a call for love, and we can begin to embrace the freedom true forgiveness brings. ~ JOHN HURST, *A Course in Miracles* study group facilitator.

You Don't Have to Die to Get to Heaven

and other true stories
on the journey back to God

Sue Pearson

RANCHO HALLELUJAH
FREEDOM PRESS
PLACERVILLE • CALIFORNIA

You Don't Have to Die
To Get to Heaven

and Other True Stories on the Journey Back to God

© 2024 Sue Pearson

Published by the author in affiliation with
Fearless Literary Services • Assisted Publishing

ISBN: 979-8-218-46303-8

Library of Congress Control Number:
2024915166

Design, Type & Production
D. Patrick Miller • Fearless Literary
www.fearlessbooks.com

Key to References

in the Complete and Annotated Edition of *A Course in Miracles*:

CE = The Complete and Annotated Edition of *A Course in Miracles*

T = Text

W = Workbook

M= Manual

Example: (CE) M-8.5:9 = Manual Section 8, paragraph 5, sentence 9

TABLE OF CONTENTS

Foreword

Sue Pearson was immersed in a bustling life as an Emmy Award-winning journalist, wife, and mother, far too busy to give thought to God or spirituality. But that changed when she went, as she says, "part way to heaven" with her dying father, who had been the north star of her life—and in the process encountered her deceased mother, who had been a cruel alcoholic. She would never be able to see her mother, or life itself, the same way again.

While Sue remained very busy and accomplished on the outside, on the inside, she was filled with a certainty that, as she puts it, "God is real and His love bigger and mightier than any concept of love I had ever had before." Along with that certainty, something had opened inside of her, and now, interwoven with all her ordinary experiences, was contact with a vast spiritual world.

That is what Sue so vividly recounts in this book. Having glimpsed light from heaven, we may assume that her life might now take on a radiant ease, but instead she seems to have been spared none of the ordinary traumas. We learn of heartbreaking revelations that lead to the end of her long marriage. We see her face the unexpected deaths of a sister and a brother, as well as face health crises of her own.

What *is* different is that at each point along the way, there is some occurrence in which the light of that other world, the light she first encountered when her father died, shines through. And that is what lifts Sue's stories above the ordinary. Again and again, something comes in that heals her heart, grants her a new perspective, or leads her to the perfect person or place.

Perhaps the main thing that happens in Sue's life when the celestial sheds its light upon the traumatic, is forgiveness. Using a term from *A Course in Miracles*, she calls it "miraculous forgiveness." This is an extreme form of forgiveness that can happen no matter what the other person has done. Miraculous forgiveness is not easy, but this is what we see Sue repeatedly reach for and touch—forgiveness of her mother, of her sister, of herself. That is where the light of the other world meets the mundane—in forgiveness. Sue admits that she is not a finished product. Rather, she is devotedly walking a path of miraculous forgiveness, which we as readers are able to walk alongside through these profound and beautiful stories.

Personally, we are so grateful Sue is finally writing openly about the strange and wonderful experiences she has had. It seems only logical that her spiritual life is at last merging with her public persona. As the head of the Circle of Atonement Story Project, Sue has been instrumental in giving voice to the spiritual experiences of others, lending her tremendous writing talents to helping other people's stories come alive and reach an audience. It has been such a joy and a pleasure to work closely with Sue in this role for several years now, and we can say without question that she is every bit the sincere, dedicated, and self-effacing person you meet in these pages.

While leading the Story Project, whenever Sue herself would contribute a story of her own, inevitably we would look at each other and say, "*These really deserve to be in a book!*" (We still can't get over how Sue reconnected with her true love!) We are so thrilled that book is here at last, and that everyone can now benefit from what we have long known is a true wisdom treasure.

Peace and gratitude,
Robert and Emily Perry

Robert Perry is the founder of the acclaimed ACIM organization known as the Circle of Atonement. He is internationally recognized as a scholar in ACIM studies. The Circle of Atonement is followed by thousands worldwide who wish to deepen their understanding of the spiritual realm. Robert's wife, Emily Perry, is the Executive Director of the Circle of Atonement. She is an experienced student and teacher of ACIM as well as a dynamic speaker and author.

ACKNOWLEDGMENTS

FIRST and foremost, I must thank my mother, Virginia Pearson, for allowing me to witness her perfection. This glimpse beyond the veil changed my life profoundly. I would have had a hard time understanding miraculous forgiveness without this holy experience. Thanks also to my father, E.O. Pearson Jr. who showed me unconditional love always and forever. I am grateful to have a best friend who turned out to be what true love is all about. I met Bill Lanterman when I was in third grade. We never forgot that blessing and are now husband and wife. Thanks to Robert and Emily Perry for bringing me into their fold at the Circle of Atonement as Editor of the Story Project. I treasure their friendship and their trust that I can bring forth from other students the beautiful lessons of *A Course in Miracles* (ACIM). The study of ACIM has brought me deep relationships with my local group: Mary Janicki, John Hurst, and Shari Anderson who also agreed to be readers for this book. They provided valuable insights as did members of my monthly writer's group: Rev. Debra Sabino, Steve Boilard, Dan Trainor, and Bob Nelson. Thank you! I am grateful for the talents of my husband's oldest son, Sam Lanterman, who is a brilliant artist and created the lilies I have used throughout this memoir as symbols of forgiveness. Thank you, D. Patrick Miller, for moving this memoir out into the world. Your many talents are appreciated.

INTRODUCTION

I WASN'T a believer, an unbeliever, or even a doubter. Was God real? I didn't know. My mind was just lazy. It was an imponderable question and would take energy away from creating a career in journalism, juggling relationships, and motherhood. I was jolted into the truth when my father died.

Growing up, my parents had been practicing protestants, first as Methodists then Episcopalians, after my baby sister died. My mother liked the grandness of Grace Episcopal Church, and she preferred the minister and the music there. My older sister, younger brother, and I all went to Sunday school until my mother's depression broke us all. Right after my little sister, Nancy, died, I think my mother thought religion might help her with her grief since that's what her father had taught as a Methodist minister. But my mother found no comfort at church no matter the denomination. Instead of comfort, she found oblivion in alcohol. My siblings and I distanced ourselves from the wreck she became, but not my father. He stood by her with love until the end.

I plowed forward with my life in the sometimes dizzying and mostly exhilarating world of broadcast journalism. My spiritual laziness had been replaced by a frantic daily pace. I became addicted to the adrenaline high of deadlines. At various times in my career, I was a reporter, a news anchor, a talk show host, and a documentary producer. I married twice and had two children plus three stepchildren. I had put together a complicated life at a time in our culture when women were being told they could have it all. Success was prized if exhausting.

My father had been my north star throughout my life. He loved me unconditionally and provided the stability and support that helped me through bad times and good times. He was my hero and my rock. He delighted in my accomplishments even though his own were far more spectacular. He had been at the forefront of the aviation industry in its infancy as an aeronautical engineer and joined the space frontier with NASA all through its developing years. He retired as Deputy Director of the Space Shuttle Program. I was so proud of him.

My relationship with my mother was a different story. She had been strict and harsh and at times cruel. It's been hard to admit this but when she died, I was glad. I didn't have to deal with her alcoholism and all the hurt it brought our family.

My father died a decade after my mother's passing and my period of spiritual laziness ended. When his diagnosis of stage 4 prostate cancer came, I fooled myself that he would overcome it. Still, he lived for four years after the doctor delivered the grim news. That final year when I knew he wasn't going to beat this cancer I began believing in God and not because I thought God was good. No, I was angry with a higher power who could dangle love in front of His constituents only to snatch it away in death. What a cruel joke. I wanted God to go away and leave us be.

Then my father died, and I had to change my mind. His death brought me an unexpected and shocking spiritual transformation. This is the story I want to tell you about and all the surprising stories that followed and continue to unfold for me as the years go on.

I became a student of A Course in Miracles in 2011. ACIM is contained in a 3-part book offering a different way to regard this world and a path to remembering who we really are. The book offers us, I believe, a bold look at truth. We are all children of God, perfect and innocent. We are not bodies having a spiritual experience but spirits having a body in a world of humans who believe they are separate beings. The Course in Miracles book consists of Text, Workbook, and Manual for Teachers. These three sections are aimed at discovering who we truly are because we have forgotten. The Text is the main introduction of principles, a workbook that offers practical exercises to enable us to see things differently, and A Manual for Teachers is meant to guide us in helping others out of darkness and into the light of who we really are as God created us.

It's important that you know my spiritual transformation happened more than a decade before I decided to become a student of A Course in Miracles. My best friend, Bill, now my husband, suggested I might like this book because of his own spiritual journey and the answers the Course provided him. He knew my journey to God had begun with my father's death. He also knew ACIM might deepen this journey. It has. I have been an ACIM student more than 13 years because the truth in the pages of this book reflect what I experienced in what is now referred to as a shared death experience (SDE) when I followed my father part way to heaven. I don't profess to completely understand all the principles of ACIM, but I do trust these words are true. I understand more as I study more. This may not be your spiritual path and even the Course itself says it is not the only path. There are many paths. I encourage you to find the one that resonates with you. The Course and many religions and spiritual doctrines stress the importance of forgiveness, love, peace, and happiness. Be wary of the paths that emphasize anger, guilt, unworthiness, hatred, and retribution.

In the Manual for Teachers within ACIM, there is a section titled **Who Are God's Teachers?** The answer: *A teacher of God is anyone who chooses to be one. His qualifications consist solely in this: Somehow, somewhere he made a deliberate choice in which he did not see his interests as apart from someone else's.* (CE)M-1:1-2

That is why I can tell you I am a teacher of God. To be sure I am not an advanced teacher of God. You could say I am a newbie teacher of God. No matter where I am on the path or where you are, what you will see in my experiences can teach you about yourself. Our earthly bodies may look different, but we are the same. I am not different because I have deepened. I am not special because I have had otherworldly events unfold in my consciousness. I am not separate from you. All of us are connected in ways many of us don't understand or want to acknowledge.

The Manual for Teachers says this about who the teachers are: *They come from all over the world. They come from all religions and from no religion. They are the ones who have answered.*

The Call is universal. (CE)M-1.2:1-4

The Manual goes on to say, *Many hear it, but few will answer. But it is all a matter of time. Everyone will answer in the end, but the end can be a long, long way off.* (CE)M-1.2:7-9

For those of us who answer the call, the Manual says, *A light has entered the darkness. It may be a single light, but it is enough.* (CE)M-1:5-6

I imagine I am one light among many who wish to bring comfort to a weary world. If in my words your worldly fears dissolve a little and make way for a measure of peace, then I have answered the call and you have heard it.

Blessings from my heart to yours. May you have peace.

CHAPTER 1

Deepening Through Miraculous Forgiveness

ACCORDING TO *A Course in Miracles,* there are two kinds of forgiveness. One is what the world considers conventional forgiveness. As ACIM puts it, *"To witness sin and yet forgive it is a paradox which reason cannot see. For it maintains what has been done to you deserves no pardon and by giving it, you grant your brother mercy but retain the proof he is not innocent."* (CE T-27.II.3)

The other kind of forgiveness is miraculous. This rests on the notion that no matter what your brother did to you or anyone there is nothing to forgive him for because he is and always will be a perfect and sinless child of God. His behavior in the world is but part of an illusion that isn't true. This is the part that is so difficult for so many people. I had a great deal of difficulty with it until I experienced miraculous forgiveness myself. It was the inspiration for the title of this book, and I use the words "Deepening through…" with each new theme as a way of telling you that everything you learn on a spiritual path has the goal of evolving or "deepening through…" to find truth. I'm not sure I could have understood miraculous forgiveness without my shared death experience. It has been a major part of my evolution back to God.

You Don't Have to Die to Get to Heaven

My whole life changed when I followed my father to heaven and experienced a glimpse of the divine. Up to this point in my life, I had not been a believer in God. Neither was I an unbeliever. I was content living my life without any kind of faith in a life beyond this earthly realm. I was busy with my career as a journalist and my roles as wife and mother. My father's death turned my world upside down. I had a shared death experience accompanying him part way on his divine journey.

Many people doubt the truth of near-death experiences (NDEs) citing so-called scientific explanations — patients near death with hallucinations due to lack of oxygen or having other brain chemical changes when death is near that produce false images. But I was not near death myself when my father passed over, neither was I impaired by drugs or alcohol or anything else that might cause false perceptions. What I experienced that night when everything changed felt like the TRUTH. All else in this world revealed itself as illusory. Here's how this extraordinary vision unfolded:

I knew my father had advanced prostate cancer for which there was no cure, but I refused to accept that he would die. He was my lifetime hero, my fount of unconditional love, and I could not imagine my life without him in it. Certainly, I was troubled by his illness, but I fooled myself into thinking there could be a treatment that would allow him many more years on earth.

One morning as I readied myself for work putting on my makeup at the sink in the bathroom, something shocking happened. My husband had already left for work and my children were in school, so the house was unusually quiet. As I applied my lipstick the entire master bathroom was enveloped with a fragrance so strong, so unmistakable it shocked me to my core. It was the unique scent of my mother. I didn't know on a conscious level what my mother had smelled like but subconsciously the connection of the baby to the mother was cemented by smell. I knew without a doubt that my departed mother was trying to reach me. My knees buckled so that I had to sit down. What did she want to tell me? Without resistance, I opened myself to receiving her message. She told me three things:

1. Your father is going to die very soon,
2. There is nothing you can do to change this, and
3. I am going to help him.

And then the scent of her withdrew quite suddenly.

My mother had not been a very loving presence in my life. When my sister and I were young she hit us when we misbehaved. She didn't just use her hand to deliver a spanking. She struck us with sticks, hairbrushes, wooden paddles, and more. We were afraid of her anger towards us. She was frequently drunk and sometimes disappeared for periods of time. We'd find her in a closet with the door closed or some other odd place. I remember her passed out most days when I came home from school, but she always put herself back together in time to prepare a nice dinner for my father. She was always attentive to him but at times neglectful of her children.

Her mean-spiritedness reached a towering hatred towards me one afternoon when I asked if I could visit a friend. Her smile curled into a sneer as she spoke to me.

"Dear Susan, aren't you the lucky one to feel loved and cared for every day of your life." Her voice got low as she snarled, "It's a lie, little girl. I have never loved you, not then, not now, not ever. Now, leave me alone!"

I was devastated. Was this the truth? Even if it wasn't, what mother would ever want to deliver such a hurtful message to her child? I couldn't stop the tears for hours, days even. In fact, as I grew into adulthood, I cried over the memory of those words many times.

Some years later when she died from liver and kidney failure due to chronic alcoholism, I did not shed a tear. I was relieved none of us would have to deal with her again. My father, however, always loved her. Even when his children urged him to divorce her, he told us he would never leave her.

Then ten years after her death she came for a visit. Her scent had heralded her presence. She delivered an unexpected and unwelcome message to me about my father's impending death. Was she singling me out yet again for her uncommon cruelty? This felt very different. On some level, I knew she had delivered the truth to me, and it broke through all my defenses. I sat there and sobbed for a very long time.

The following week I had a vision of experiencing my life flashing before me in fast rewind showing me that every decision I ever made was perfect for my journey and totally understandable. I never made a "good" or "bad" decision. The experience felt like a kind of purging of shame, regret, and unworthiness. All things were as they should be, and I need not second guess any decision I ever made.

Two weeks later my father was hospitalized, and the siblings and grandchildren gathered by his side in Ft. Lauderdale, Florida where he had lived for many years.

On the third day of our vigil, we could see that dad was deteriorating. He floated in and out of a coma state for much of the day. When it was time to go back to his condominium for the night, I lingered at my father's hospital bedside.

"I love you, Dad."

And in a strong, clear voice he answered back.

"I love you too, Sue."

The children and the grandchildren settled in for the night. My sister and I shared a king-sized bed in one of the two condos my father owned. I couldn't sleep but I was not anxious or upset, just quiet and calm. I could hear my sister snoring quietly beside me and knew she was sleeping.

And then my mother's foretelling unfolded in sights and senses I didn't know I had.

In the stillness of the night, from my father's condo, I saw him in his hospital bed with a gathering light coming to the upper right side of the bed. He was very frail. The advancing light was beyond words, inviting, intense, pure, a light unlike any I had seen before. I became aware of movement within the light and was drawn to that as it pulsed. I soon saw that my mother was in the light, was part of the light, and that this was the light of life itself, the light of God. She was more beautiful than any woman I had ever seen before. There was a purity and innocence in her essence. When I saw her this way there was, in an instant, complete forgiveness for anything I might have perceived as hurtful about her behavior on this earth. When I saw her in the light, she was holy and I knew this was the truth about her, not at all how she seemed on earth.

Many years later I would read this passage in a spiritual book entitled *A Course in Miracles*:

> Can you imagine how beautiful those you forgive will look to you? In no fantasy have you ever seen anything so lovely. Nothing you see here, sleeping or waking, comes near such loveliness, and nothing will you value like unto this, nor hold so dear. Nothing that you remember that made your heart seem to sing with joy has ever brought you even a little part of the happiness this sight will bring you. For you will see the Son of God.
> (CE)T-17.II:1-5

When I read this in the Course twenty years after my father's death, I knew it was the truth because I had experienced it that holy day I saw my mother help my father pass over to heaven. When I saw her in that divine light nearing my father's bedside, she was the most beautiful woman I had ever seen before. Now my mother was attractive in this earth realm, but in heaven she was indescribably beautiful. Think of all the female celebrities we have come to think of as beautiful: Angelina Jolie, Margot Robbie, Elizabeth Taylor, Marilyn Monroe, and many others. My mother's beauty far exceeded any of them. My heart did sing with joy as I saw her in heaven just as the Course said it would. I was looking at the child of God!

I knew in that awareness that God is real and His love bigger and mightier than any concept of love I had ever had before. In the earth realm, I could not conceive of a love like this but in the light beside my father's hospital bed, I understood a love beyond earthly perception. I also understood from my mother and God that we are here on this earth for one purpose — to love one another. We have made this life journey on earth so complicated as humans, but in the divine light, I understood everything was truly simple. There was no sense of time in this vision, only an imparting of pure truth all at once. I saw my mother reach out to my father and lift him into her light, cradling him in her arms. Then the light began to fade and disappear from my vision. I then saw with my body's eyes that I was in the bed in my father's condo where I had been before the vision, my sister next to me still snoring. I glanced at the clock. It was just before midnight.

In an hour or two the phone rang, and it was the hospital telling me that my father had died. The nurse asked if we wanted to come view his body before they took it to the hospital morgue. So, at about 2 a.m. we all (my sister and her daughter, my brother Jon, my daughter Christine, and I) got in the car and drove to the hospital. We gathered around his body and said prayers of thanksgiving for his love in our lives. A nurse came into the room, and I asked her if she knew when my father had passed on. She said she had come in to check on him a little before midnight and could see he was near death. She left him alone and returned at 12:15 to find that he had died. Then I knew that my vision was real, and I began to sob at the sudden knowing of so many things: Mother had said she would help my father and she did. She was holy and pure and a child of God. God is love and love is all. Our purpose in this realm is to love each other. Faith in the truth had come to me like a bolt of lightning, a true vision, and I was forever changed.

The next day my brother Jon and I went to a local restaurant for brunch. It was a popular place and sure enough, the line to get seated was down the sidewalk and around the corner. Jon and I had nowhere else to be, so we found the end of the line and waited. Minutes passed and a lovely young woman with a hostess sign on her blouse approached us. She took my hand and said, "Follow me."

"Is this OK to cut in front of all these people?" I asked her.

"Yes, it's absolutely fine," she replied.

She guided us to a table inside the restaurant. As we sat down we wondered how many people wanted to clobber us for jumping ahead of everyone in line.

The beautiful hostess said, "My name is Virginia and I am here to help you."

Jon and I looked at each other, both of us in shocked surprise. I said, "Our mother's name was Virginia. It's not a common name these days."

"Well, I believe I am here to represent her," said the lovely lady, flashing an exquisite smile.

As she turned to leave, Jon whispered to me, "Can you believe what just happened?"

"Yes, I can."

What followed my heavenly vision was a two-year period of what I have come to understand was grace. I was in tears almost every day from the joy of the world I was seeing with new eyes. I saw the preciousness of everyone including high school students in a class I taught who had been deemed "troublesome" by the school administration. I joined Trinity Episcopal Cathedral in Sacramento. My son Evan and I attended Sunday services each week. I cried at the beauty I saw in the people and their rituals.

I told only a handful of people about my huge vision even though I wanted to shout to everyone, "There is nothing to fear in this world. There is no death!" I realized I could not give anyone the divine experience that changed my life and that some people would think I was at best quirky and at worst insane.

After my father's death, my sister became estranged from me. I did not understand why she despised me, but she made it clear she did not want me in her life though I tried in letters and phone calls to reconnect. I was very distraught by her hateful attitude. I didn't tell my sister about my vision because she was in such a troubled state my story would not have been helpful.

She neither wanted nor could accept any comfort from me.

I went to a healing service at Trinity with the laying on of hands. I had been quite troubled by my sister's feelings towards me and had prayed she would come to her senses. At this healing service, I decided to change my prayer. I asked God to help me surrender my pain about this relationship and accept my sister's decision to cut me out of her life. I waited in the line leading to the altar for my turn to kneel there and let a healing helper lay hands on me. I did not expect anything to happen to me immediately, but it did. As this lovely church woman put both of her hands on my head, I felt a gentle warmth surround my head, a feeling of heat and light that filled my mind with awareness and took away all the pain I had felt about my sister. I experienced a miraculous, instantaneous healing. I left the church feeling a great lifting of a burden and a beautiful sense of peace.

It has been twenty years since all of this happened to me. Here are all the things I gained:

- Rock solid faith in God
- No more fear of death
- More loving and accepting of my brothers and sisters
- An understanding of the importance of forgiveness
- A knowing that love is all that is real
- A deep gratitude to my Creator and all that is holy, more joy, more peace, more contentment.

This is but a short list. As I live this earth experience to its conclusion, the insights keep unfolding and enriching me. And I believe my amazing transformation has touched many loved ones in ways they might not even be aware of or could express in words. After all, I have learned there are senses beyond our physical bodies that can guide us to truth.

My two-year state of grace slowly faded but the life-changing foundation of my vision remains. Forgiveness is the key to heaven. When I understood the truth of who my mother is in God's eyes—perfect, innocent, and holy—nothing she had done on earth mattered at all to me. It was as if it had all been undone. Thank you, sweet Mother, and thank you dear God for the precious gifts forgiveness brings.

A passage in *A Course in Miracles* affirms what I know to be the truth of my experience.

All this beauty will rise to bless your sight as you look upon the world with forgiving eyes. For forgiveness literally transforms vision, and lets you see the real world reaching quietly and gently across chaos and removing all illusions that had twisted your perception and fixed it on the past. (CE)T-17.II.6:1-2

Years later my sister and I reconciled. I had survived a life-threatening health crisis with a brain aneurysm (more on that later) and I suppose my sister thought she might not see me again. She flew out to San Francisco from Atlanta, Georgia and I met her at Grace Cathedral in the city. There is an exquisite labyrinth just beyond the doorway into the sanctuary. Walking the labyrinth is an ancient tradition. It may look like a maze, but it isn't. There is only one path to the center and then back out again. There is no way to get lost so there is no worry about finding the right path. There is only the one, but it does twist and turn through the circle. Without the worry of getting lost, you are free to meditate or pray as you walk along.

So, I began our walk on this day, my sister behind me. What I noticed was symbolic and remarkable. At times because of all the turns, my sister and I were very far apart, almost at opposite sides of the circle. At other times we were so close we could reach out and touch each other's hands.

It was like this in life. Sometimes we were very far apart, she in Atlanta, me in Sacramento, California, and at other times like this one we were very close, physically able to touch. We were at times distant and then close emotionally through the years as well. Her total disconnection from me had troubled me until I accepted whatever it was she was going through. Now in this beautiful church, she was hugging me and telling me how much she loved me. I asked her why she had turned her back on me. Her only answer was, "I was not well." I think she was referring to a deep depression.

To my mind, my sister's life began to change dramatically when her first marriage came apart. She seemed more volatile. Perhaps that volatility is what propelled her to go back to school and earn a master's degree. At the time she was a single mom raising a young daughter and trying to find her footing in a new career direction. She married for a second time and when that one began to fall apart, she fell apart too. She landed in a psychiatric hospital and was diagnosed as bipolar disorder. Medication and her tenacity pulled her back into the world.

As a single woman, she had a series of troubled relationships with men. She told me she worried that she was not a suitable partner for a love relationship. But she seemed to find some stability with one man, and they moved in together. I met him a couple of times and he seemed like a nice guy. Then at one of my visits, I noticed how controlling and strident she was becoming with him. He seemed surprisingly patient with her, but I think he was at the same time looking for a way out of the relationship. He left suddenly and she was devastated.

Looking back, I think this was a major trigger for the manic/depressive stage she was moving into. When she came out to California to visit me she seemed fully manic—buying expensive things for me and my daughter and indulging herself as well. I don't know how long this phase lasted but in time she crashed. I thought this could be a happy time for her. She moved to a fancy new neighborhood in Atlanta, and things seemed to be going well, but they weren't really. When I visited her in her new home, I could see how depressed she was. She didn't want to go out of her house, she wasn't eating much and was losing weight.

Let me turn your attention back to forgiveness because what happened next was difficult. Indeed, the trauma many people have experienced in this earth realm seems unforgivable. But I believe our ability to forgive everyone everything is paramount to our journey back to God. Yes, even murderers, sexual predators, and tyrants are, in spirit, as God created them — children of God. As ACIM says, "God does not forgive because He has never condemned." (CE)W-46:1

And so, I had to face what seemed unforgivable.

Broken Hearts

Oh God! I must have uttered this anguished plea a dozen times, maybe more. *Oh God, please no! Oh God, this can't be! Oh God, how could she?*

My sister's executive assistant had called me on my cell phone. She had never called me before. "Sue, if you are driving, please pull over to a safe place and then I can tell you what has happened."

Well, I knew this was not going to be good news, but I couldn't imagine the depth of the hurt she was about to deliver. I pulled into a parking lot. "OK, what's up?"

"Your sister killed herself."

Oh God!...

Darkness descended like black clouds of an atmospheric river releasing a torrent of unrelenting pain. I knew my sister had been depressed but suicide was unthinkable. Years ago, she had said she would never forgive her former husband for committing suicide. He shot himself. My sister knew the debilitating hurt that settled into loved ones left behind to cope.

Now she had done the same thing, taking her own life. She hung herself from a dramatic 3-story entryway in her home. *Oh God! What a sight!*

My sister had been diagnosed as bipolar some years before. It helped explain her dramatic mood swings and sometimes odd behavior.

Medication seemed to help but not this time. The last time I saw her was at her home in Atlanta about 6 months before her mental crash, I had urged her to find a good psychiatrist. She promised she would.

Weeks before, my sister had called me as I was driving to San Francisco from my home in the foothills east of Sacramento, California. I debated whether to take the call. We had a long history of volatility in our relationship. More than once she admitted to me and her friends that she had not treated me well when we were growing up. We got along better in our later years until she slid into critic mode, listing my faults and failures. I loved her anyway. There were times I could see her inner beauty. Other times I just kept my distance.

Looking back, I can see the roots of her love/hate relationship with me — resentment. My mother was a master of the backhanded compliment, and she was particularly hard on my sister. "Oh, sweetie, you should be glad you got the brains, not the beauty. Sue only got the good looks," she said with a laugh. Though by now I knew of my mother's innocence and perfection from my shared death experience, in the earth realm my mother's brand of discipline had been quite harsh, and my sister bore the brunt of it. She was often hit with not just a hand but a hairbrush across the face, a wooden paddle to her behind, or sticks whipping her legs. I mostly kept my mouth shut and avoided some, but not all, of this abuse.

I don't know exactly how she descended into the hell that was her world in those final months. I don't want to point blame at other people or events. I know that what happens to each of us happens within ourselves. After her boyfriend left her, she started having trouble at work. Her board of directors asked her to leave. And then, looking for love, she joined a questionable dating app online and connected with what turned out to be a con man wanting money from her. I am not sure if she sent him any, but she told me she had wrecked her financial security.

At the same time, she began calling me and sending me emails describing what a failure I had been as a mother. Her rants were very disturbing even though I knew what she was saying was not true. I had loving relationships with both my daughter and my son with not a hint of crisis in their lives from bad mothering. Yet my sister persisted in her criticisms.

I told her to stop calling. I advised her to seek counseling. She just grew angrier. So, when she called my cell phone that day on the way to the Bay area, I almost ignored it. But I picked up. She apologized. She said she needed me to promise something. She wanted my word I would attend a loved one's wedding. I told her I worried about her becoming unhinged at the wedding and making a public display of her anger towards me. I said I wanted no part of that kind of disturbance on a day that should be the biggest and best celebration of love. On the phone, there was no fight left in my sister which I thought was unusual. She begged me to be at the wedding. At the time I didn't quite understand the urgency behind this plea. I told her I would seriously consider attending the wedding. She said, "Thank you. I love you."

Now I know what was behind the urgency of her request. She wasn't going to be at the wedding. She was going to end her life.

After she killed herself, I flew to Atlanta to try and help settle her affairs. I walked through the front door of my sister's condo expecting to be hit with very dark energy. But the energy seemed neutral to me. My sister's presence was gone along with the anguish she carried. In her home office, I was shocked to see files neatly laid out on her desktop showing that all the bills were paid up. Her will was there too along with lists of important contacts. It was clear that my sister had planned this desperate act. Upstairs in the main living area everything was tidy — dishes washed, countertops cleaned, nothing out of place, not a hint of the disarray in my sister's mind. All this just deepened my anguish. How could she have planned this knowing those she left behind would suffer deep trauma and unspeakable grief? I might have mustered some compassion for an act that was sudden, impulsive, spontaneous. The deliberateness of her actions was impossible to understand. Now I was angry.

When I returned to my home in California, I spent some time trying to make sense of all that had happened. Suddenly in a quiet moment alone in my living room, I saw my sister in another realm behind a shimmering transparent crystal curtain. There were several luminous beings around her just listening as my sister talked and talked non-stop. I could not hear anything she said. The crystal curtain was a soundproof barrier. My sister looked animated as she talked to the light beings. I knew I was not meant to hear what she had to say. I hoped that the beings were there to help her find her right mind and be at peace in heaven.

I knew I would find release in forgiveness, but I was not ready. First had come shock, then disbelief, reluctant acceptance, and now anger. I couldn't bring myself to think that my sister's suicide didn't matter. She had left a trail of emotional wreckage behind for family members to slog through.

I often took my problems to my dear friend Mary Witt. Mary was an ordained minister of a church that brought principles of Unity, *A Course in Miracles,* and other non-duality practices together. She was also a psychic and a medium. I had consulted with her on relationship problems, spiritual issues, and more over the years. On this day I walked into her office and announced that I wasn't there to talk about my sister.

I don't remember what I wanted to talk to her about that

day, but I will never forget what happened. After about twenty minutes Mary said, "I know you trust me and now I want to talk to you about your sister."

I surrendered not because I wanted to but because I trusted Mary. She proceeded to tell me in detail what had led to my sister's undoing. The depression had only gotten worse. The drugs the psychiatrist prescribed didn't help, they only strengthened her resolve to end the nightmare her life had become. And then she stopped eating. And that, Mary said, was the beginning of the end. Her brain became totally dysfunctional. She believed there was only one escape and she found it at the end of a rope.

As Mary spoke these words, I felt my sister's presence so strongly. It was as if we were mind to mind. I knew Mary was telling me the truth. It was coming through my sister to Mary then to me. I began to cry because now I understood what had happened, not only with her but with me. My sister and I communicated telepathically. "I can forgive you now," I said. Through her own tears, she told me how insecure and afraid she was all her life and how she covered up this vulnerability with an outer shell of toughness. I had the sudden realization that I had contributed to her poor opinion of herself with unloving thoughts and actions from our childhood on into adulthood. I had not always been kind. I said, "Please forgive me for my part in your unhappiness." I had not realized that I needed to ask her for forgiveness. Now we were both sobbing, hugging each other across the veil.

Mary said, "Well done. I was not sure you were ready, but this forgiveness is complete." Mary knew we are all connected and that what happens to one influences another. She knew how important it was to see our part of any dynamic in a relationship and forgive ourselves. Ultimately, I understood that my sister and I were no different. Had she been the only one of us who made mistakes? No, I made my share. When that realization finally enters your mind, you can release each other from guilt. Forgiveness is the big reveal. You are free to be the love God created but for a while had forgotten.

Anita Moorjani, who writes about forgiveness in her book *Dying to Be Me*, had a powerful and transformative near-death experience and writes about forgiveness in a way that resonates with me. She says, "Consider replacing the word 'forgive' with the word 'release.' In other words, instead of forgiving people, you're releasing them. You're releasing them from your life, so they no longer have a hold on you. Simply change the question from "How do I forgive them?" to "How do I release them?" And then consider yourself, love yourself, value yourself, and know you have the power to change the dynamics of any situation." I think this "releasing" should include letting go of blame, shame, and guilt. This to me is as close as many of us get to miraculous forgiveness.

Here's another view from *A Course in Miracles* — a prayer. *I give you to the Holy Spirit, as part of myself. I know that you will be released, unless I want to use you to imprison myself. In the name of my freedom, I will your release, because I recognize that we will be released together.* (CE)T-15.XI:5-7

A Course in Miracles goes even further, telling us that forgiveness is the acceptance that nothing happened because this earth realm is a dream—an illusion. That's quite a stretch for many of us, especially those of us touched by trauma.

My view is that while I am in this "earth dream" I will find my higher self by seeing my brother/sister as no different than myself, the holy child of God. Not only does she need forgiveness, but my forgiveness of myself is of equal importance and will happen as I forgive her.

I love you, Sister. I love you, Sue.

CHAPTER 2

Deepening Through Mystical Moments

Dr. Bruce Greyson, Professor of Psychiatry at the University of Virginia says "Near Death Experiences [NDEs] do not necessarily promote any one particular religious or spiritual tradition over others, but they do foster general spiritual growth both in the experiencers and in human society at large."

I think this helps explain why so many who have had NDEs or SDEs continue to have deep spiritual growth in the years that follow their initial experiences. We become open-minded about events that can't be explained in worldly terms. In other words, there is much more to sense than just what we see and hear with our body's eyes and ears.

William Peters, psychotherapist, and Founder of the Shared Crossing Project has been studying shared death experiences for over a decade. He and his colleagues have interviewed thousands of people who have experienced SDE's. Many of those accounts are found in his book *At Heaven's Door*.

"We have found that over 50% (of experiencers) will have an ongoing relationship with the departed loved one, usually a post-death visitation, a post-death synchronicity. I used to think the synchronicities were way out there, and I wouldn't touch them at all as a researcher, but then we started getting all these incredible synchronistic things like cloud formations, and accounts of electronic clocks flashing key dates, anniversaries, birthdays, and time of death. This all goes into this ongoing relationship that people feel they're having with their departed loved ones," according to Peters.

When my mind was more fully opened after my shared death experience, I found I was also more open to experience the unexplainable. The first time it was discerning the scent of my mother. As an adult, I was unaware that my mother had a unique scent, but I think babies know this about their mothers. My own mother's unique scent flooded the room as I applied my makeup for the day. It was so overpowering I could not ignore it or pretend I didn't know where this had come from. My deceased mother needed to tell me something important and she knew I would remember her scent from my time with her as an infant. I can't explain how she was able to reach me this way. She just did. I listened. She told me telepathically that my father was going to die very soon, that I could do nothing to change this, and finally, she told me she would help him cross over.

There have been many other unexplainable sensory experiences since that first one. When my best friend, and now husband, Bill came to join me at my home in California I introduced him to my ACIM study group. He had studied the Course for many years, but this was the first time he had studied with other like-minded people. As we were walking along the path to the front door of the host's home we were overwhelmed with the smell of roses. We thought the rose bushes we passed were the source of this fragrance, so we stopped to smell the blooms. It was wintertime. There was no fragrance to these roses. We were puzzled. We noticed the intense fragrance of roses that followed us into the house. When we stepped into the living room another woman in the group expressed great surprise. "Where are the roses? The whole room is filled with the smell of roses, but I don't see any," she said. Two others in the group said they didn't smell anything at all. Bill, this other woman, and I continued for a while to experience this intense smell of roses.

We still aren't sure why this happened, but my newfound faith told me it was a blessing. Perhaps Bill's deceased mother, who loved gardening and roses most of all, had bestowed her beloved son with a sign she was happy for him to join this group. Sometimes we just accept what is happening without knowing why.

At other times I have known the why. Before my sister's death, we jointly experienced the unexplainable. Please join me on this next journey into mystical moments.

Juicy Fruit Gum

My mother hated the smell of Juicy Fruit chewing gum. It had a sickly, sweet fruity aroma. As a young girl, my sister Margie loved it but not so much for the flavor or smell. Chewing it was a playful way to get revenge on our mother.

Now in our 60s, Margie and I went to a spiritual retreat at a Catholic retreat center in Northern California. It was called

Women's Spiritual Spa, and it was meant to honor, bless, and provide respite to women. It is always a sold-out event at the retreat center. Every moment of this 3-day retreat felt like an embrace to us. We left feeling so well taken care of and serene. On the drive back to my house my sister reminded me of something we liked to do as children.

When my mother was driving. Margie would open a big pack of Juicy Fruit gum and hand me half of the sticks. Mother couldn't see what we were up to in the back seat, but she soon found out. Each of us put every stick of that sickly, sweet gum in our mouths and chewed it into a big soft wad. With our mouths open and lips smacking we sent clouds of Juicy Fruit smell towards the driver of the car. Our mother would groan and gag. We loved making her sick. It was our way of exacting some small revenge on a mother who was often domineering and harsh, but we all laughed about the smell and the gagging, even Mother.

Mother had died some 25 years ago and now her two grown daughters were remembering a silly moment from our childhood. Suddenly the car I was driving these many years later was filled with that old familiar smell of Juicy Fruit gum. I was astonished—I thought I might be imagining the aroma. "Margie, do you smell something?"

"Of course. It's the smell of Juicy Fruit gum," she said.

"Don't you find that amazing?" I asked.

Margie just grumbled on about our mother's meanness while I sent Mom a prayer thanking her for joining us in the car this day for a loving little joke between us.

At another time a health crisis brought mystical moments when I thought perhaps my time on this earth had run out. It turns out I had unexpected company — God and His angels.

Aneurysm Emergency

I had been having the worst headaches of my life. My then-husband told me the headaches were likely hormone-related and if I was really concerned, I should make an appointment with my primary care doctor. Fortunately, I already had made the appointment. She booked an MRI for me which showed an aneurysm in my brain just behind my left eye. I went in for emergency surgery immediately at our local hospital. But on the way to the hospital, I called my cameraman.

At the time I was a broadcast journalist and just happened to be working on a public television documentary on stroke. With the terrible pain in my head, I struggled to help my editor wrap up this program. When it was finished, I was frustrated that we were 45 seconds too short for the strict PBS rules on program length. I had no energy to craft a new section, so I told my editor to just slow the credits down and add some music at the end. Not ideal but we would satisfy the guidelines. So, when I called my cameraman on the way to the hospital, I was thinking perhaps we could capture an exciting new treatment for brain bleeds even if I had no idea if it could be done on me or even if I would live through this crisis.

At the hospital, it was determined that the particular size

and shape of my brain aneurysm made it perfect for this new kind of less-invasive surgery. A neuro-interventionalist would snake a catheter from an artery in my groin up into the bulging vessel in my brain. Then he would thread platinum wires through the catheter which would fan out into a slinky-like shape when it reached the bulging vessel. It took six of these platinum wires to fill the aneurysm and essentially pack it so it couldn't burst. The doctor explained to me this was a life-and-death emergency but since he had never had a patient in this condition be so calm, he would allow me to remain awake if I so desired. I did. I thought if this was the end of my life on earth, I didn't want to miss a second of it.

Even though the pain in my head was very intense I found myself able to simply notice it rather than be in any great suffering at this very fragile time when my life hung in the balance. I was overcome with a calm greater than anything I could have imagined. I surrendered everything to a higher power and knew that I would be OK no matter the outcome. I knew God was very near and that I would be taken care of if I died and taken care of if I lived through this medical emergency.

While the doctors and nurses worked on me, I could hear quite clearly the voices of several friends of mine who had gathered in a waiting room down the hall. I could hear my husband and his nurse in the room next door. They were all expressing great concern for me, and it was comforting for me to know they cared enough to stand vigil. I have read that other people who are in life-and-death emergencies can have extraordinary experiences. Some describe an out-of-body experience—of leaving their bodies and being able to view the scene from above. Others have described unusual or heightened senses and that is what I believe happened to me. I have no doubt I received comfort from God who let me know I would be OK no matter what. I had no fear of death at that moment because I was sustained by the peace of God. I was able to receive messages from people I loved who were at the hospital but not within any normal hearing range. I don't understand how that happens. I just know that it does.

When the coil procedure, as it is called, was finished, I called out, "Did you get it all?" The doctor thought I was talking about successfully plugging the aneurysm, but I was talking to my cameraman, who had abruptly ended a day of skiing in the nearby mountains to join me and videotape my procedure.

"Got it, Sue!" he replied. It was a moment of mirth in an otherwise tense life-and-death situation.

It took me a couple of months to recover. At first, I found it difficult to find the right words for simple things. A "pencil" might come out of my mouth as a "knife" even though in my mind I knew this wasn't correct. Another deficit was just listening. If only one person was talking, I could hear and understand. If there were two or more people, I could not process a thing anyone said. But all these minor problems disappeared after a few months.

I was able to get together with my editor and insert a short section in our documentary on stroke about the miraculous new coil procedure for repairing aneurysms. It filled the 45 seconds we had been missing and added a punch of drama to our program.

That spring I won a regional Emmy for this program, which was distributed nationally to PBS stations across the country.

I was invited to appear on ABC's Good Morning America to talk about my amazing experience. They headlined this live interview "Life imitates art."

Was all this just a coincidence? In my mind, it could not have been anything but a miracle.

Terror at Terezin

I never thought I would be a tourist in a Nazi concentration camp but there I was at Terezin. The tour guide was leading a group of people curious about what this place had been during World War II. I hadn't wanted to be there. I thought seeing it would be grim, but it was part of a package of activities included in my stay in Prague.

I was enchanted with Prague. From the time I got off the airplane and into this very old city, I felt I had time-traveled back to the 13th century. It is known as the city of spires because of all the old buildings with these distinctive roofs over the entire skyline. These structures date back centuries and have been carefully preserved and maintained to this day. It is the capital of the Czech Republic today and was, in ancient times, the capital of the Kingdom of Bohemia. I walked the narrow streets and crossed the beautiful Charles Bridge stopping to buy a souvenir from a vendor or two. In Old Town Square I wandered through art galleries and gift shops, delighting at a set of red crystal wine glasses engraved with horses. I bought them and arranged for shipping back to California. I fell in love with Prague.

When it was time to get on a bus and travel thirty miles to the north I was concerned. I knew I wouldn't be able to fall in love with Terezin. It too had been an ancient city but during WWII Nazi Germany took it over and turned it into a concentration camp. Terezin itself wasn't a death camp but rather a place to hold prisoners for a short time before being sent to notorious Treblinka or Auschwitz.

More than 150,000 Jews and 15,000 children were sent to Terezin during the war. Living conditions in the town were terrible but Hitler had an idea that would fuel the propaganda campaign and fool the world. When a group of Red Cross officials demanded to visit Terezin to see how the prisoners were being treated, Hitler ordered the town be turned into an idyllic village with lovely shops, museums, concert venues, and happy Jews. The Red Cross inspectors were not allowed to speak to the townspeople and what they saw convinced them the Jews were being treated well. It was a ruse. The Jews were prisoners in an outrageous plot to convince the rest of the world the Nazis were benevolent guardians.

When I visited this place more than two decades ago, I was saddened by the emptiness of the streets and the knowledge that in those long-ago days when it seemed to be thriving with people and children, arts, and entertainment, it was all just a terrible lie.

Next to the empty town was an empty prison. It had been a prison long before the World Wars and the Nazis found it a convenient place to lock up political prisoners. Our tour guide walked us through the main doors and down narrow corridors. The place was dingy and of course, housed only ghosts of the people who had been here. I know this because something unexpected and horrifying happened to me when we were invited to look at the cells. In the first block of cells we looked at, I felt distinctly disturbed. Anxiety was creeping into my mind. I supposed I was thinking about how awful it would have been to be locked up in this place. But things got worse for me. The next block of cells we were told was for solitary confinement. Members of our tour group walked into some of the small, now empty rooms. The first one I came to brought me more and even deeper emotional disturbance. I was suddenly filled with terrible fear. I began to shake and sweat. Still, I walked on to the next room. At the doorway, I was overwhelmed with abject terror. I couldn't speak. My knees felt weak. I could not walk through that doorway. I knew I was feeling the energy of what resided in that prison cell those many years before. What those prisoners experienced was worse than any hell I could imagine but now felt at a visceral level.

I gasped when the tour guide told us he was going to take us into a large courtyard where prisoners were either hung from gallows or lined up against a wall and shot to death. Just hearing about it made me think I might faint. I couldn't imagine anything worse than what I had experienced in the solitary confinement cells and what happened when we arrived at the courtyard shocked me to the depth of my soul.

I felt peace. I stood for the longest time looking at the wall where people were lined up and shot. I had thought I would feel their fear, their horror at what was about to happen. But the energy I sensed in this place was freedom, an escape from hell, peace, and gratitude the nightmare would all be over.

The visit to Terezin had left me drained and exhausted but now in this courtyard, I felt relieved that hell had ended there. I hadn't known the history of Terezin when I started the tour. I didn't know what I might experience there. I was shaken by this unexpected sensory experience.

New age science might describe what happened to me as psychometry. This is a process whereby an experiencer learns facts or gets impressions about a person through contact with an object or, in this case, a place. It emerged as a kind of science in 1842 when Dr. Joseph Rodes Buchanan came up with the word "psychometry." He believed that all things give off an emanation or energy. Today the term has been folded into a category called extrasensory perception.

I know that I have developed sensitivities allowing me to "see" without using my eyes. It is a kind of mind vision that picks up signals from others whether they exist in this earth realm or beyond. It is a deepening that took me by surprise. *A Course in Miracles* offers a view that resonates with me:

Communication is not limited to the small range of channels the world recognizes... Who transcends these limits (on communication) in any way is merely becoming more natural. He is doing nothing special, and there is no magic in his accomplishments. Those who have developed "psychic" powers have merely let some of the limitations they had laid upon their minds be lifted.
(CE) M-25.2:2-6

The Course agrees that the laying aside of some of these communication limits can be useful.

Any ability that anyone develops has the potential for good. To this, there is no exception. And the more unusual and unexpected the power, the greater its potential usefulness. (CE) M-25.6:1-3

What the Terezin experience showed me was that death became a release for the prisoners who were shot or hanged. I imagine Jesus felt that release as he hung from the cross. His resurrection demonstrated for all of us that death is not an end to life but a doorway to the eternal.

Enchantment Encounter

Some might say what I saw was a ghost, or an angel, or a spirit guide. Whatever it was, I know it most certainly was a healing force. It happened at a resort in Sedona, Arizona called The Enchantment. Sedona is well known by spiritual seekers as a place where energy forces gather in vortexes to aid in all kinds of healing — spirit, mind, and/or body. The early people of this land were Native Americans, and many tribes are still active here: the Hopi, Navajo, Tonto, Apache, and Yavapai. But one spot became known as the origin of the Yavapai Apache Nation. According to Native legend, Boynton Canyon was the place where First Woman gave birth to humans. It was and still is considered a sacred space with a balance of masculine and feminine energy for healing. The developers and managers at the Enchantment have tried to honor and protect Boynton Canyon as sacred land, but tribe members today say there is still tension over the handling of their history and the need to ask permission to visit or hold ceremonies at their ancestral sacred spaces.

I went to the Enchantment resort with my second husband who had been invited to attend a professional conference. I should have been happy to be staying in such a beautiful place, but I was miserable. I was ashamed of who I had become—someone not-so-nice. Up to this point in my life, I think most people would have described me as personable, steady, and easy-going. Those qualities disappeared when I had to interact with one person in particular — my husband's ex-wife. She never seemed to miss an opportunity to be insulting and hurtful in her dealings with both me and my husband. I was doing the best I could to handle a stressful career as a broadcast journalist, a home, a husband, and five yours-mine-and-ours children. The ex-wife would bring her three children over to our house at all hours when they were misbehaving, or she needed a babysitter. We always took them in on these unscheduled visits. She often swore at us when she dropped off the children and told me they hated me. I knew they didn't, but it hurt me to see the children having to deal with her tirades.

After years of this kind of abuse, I yielded to my darker side. I met every insult of hers with an insult of my own. When she delivered the kids with bags of dirty clothes, I found a way to strike back. When it was time to send the children to her house, I put their clean clothes in plastic bags carefully slit at the bottom so that all the clothes would fall out into the street when she picked up the bags. She was furious! I was glad.

Was I happy? No, I had turned myself into a nasty, re-active, petty mess all because of my reaction to one difficult person. I wanted to change but didn't know if I could on my own. Now I was in this sacred place, yearning for a way out of the darkness I had created. I went for a hike by myself in Boynton Canyon. I was struck by the tranquility of the natural environment and amazed at the ancient ruins in the caves of the canyon where Natives had lived so long ago. When I neared the resort buildings on the way back to my room, I spotted a large domed rock. I climbed up to the top and sat there alone with thoughts of unworthiness. The tears came in torrents. "Please God," I prayed, "help me find my higher self. This negativity I feel is poisoning me. I don't want to be the kind of person who relishes retribution. Please help me let go of hatred, anxiety, and fear." After a long time, I stopped crying and just sat there quietly.

I pulled myself together and joined my husband for a lovely dinner and evening entertainment. Hours later in our room, it was time to get some sleep before the busy next day of touring vortexes began.

Sometime in the middle of the night, I was awakened by the sound of rhythmic drumming. My husband was asleep, but I was now wide awake. I thought it was curious that some ceremony with Native drumming would be taking place at 3 a.m. on the grounds of the Enchantment. I went into the bathroom and opened the window there to see if that was where the sounds were coming from. The sound was not outside at all. The sound was somewhere in the room. I surveyed the room to see if there were speakers on the walls or a radio on. Nothing was being broadcast. I was shocked and now frightened that I could not find the source of the drumming. It seemed to me to be a Shamanic kind of steady, repeating rhythm, not loud but persistent. I considered that this might be a supernatural occurrence because I could not identify the source of the sound.

This thought scared me, and I scrambled to get back in bed where I thought I could escape the unexplainable. I could not. There was more to this experience and what happened next was shocking. I became aware that my fear was intensifying with the steady beat of the drum. All that poisonous negativity I wanted to get rid of was rising to the surface of my awareness. And then suddenly a Native American man appeared in the room. He was wearing a black breechcloth and deerskin moccasins. He was bare-chested with a slim but muscular build. His face was smooth and unwrinkled, suggesting he was a young man. He wore a black headband with one feather to the side, his long hair pulled back into a single braid.

Was he real or a figment of my imagination? I had taken no mind-altering substances, yet I could clearly see a Native man in my room. Strangely enough, I was not frightened by his presence. He walked ever so quietly over to my side of the bed and lay down beside me. I sensed he was there for some purpose that had to do with me. I didn't know what that was, but I accepted that something was supposed to happen. All those negative feelings I had wanted to lose had heightened during the drumming. This Native spirit lay silently next to me with his arms at his sides. The drumming continued. I didn't think once about awakening my husband. I knew something important was happening for myself alone. The Native spirit rose from the bed and then disappeared.

I can't remember if I slept for a while afterward. I do remember that when the drumming stopped all that anxiety and negativity within me receded like an ocean wave at low tide. I felt different, unburdened. What had happened during the night was so shocking to me that I didn't dare mention it to anyone for fear they would think I was crazy. I did ask my husband if he had heard any drumming and he said he hadn't heard a thing.

When I returned home, I wondered if what happened to me was an answer to my prayer on the rock where I had wept and asked for divine help. I took some time to examine my current feelings toward my husband's ex-wife. I could tell I was no longer filled with hatred or dread over our next encounter. I was surprised that for the first time, I felt compassion for her.

Her behavior toward me seemed to come from her feelings of insecurity. Not once, after my Native spirit helped me by carrying my burdens away, did I behave badly toward this woman again.

In fact, years later she and I had a reconciliation, complete with mutual forgiveness. I never thought this would happen, but we both acknowledged our uncivil, unkind behavior and apologized for it.

It has taken me so long to be brave enough to tell this story. I knew something miraculous had happened at the Enchantment, but the experience just wouldn't have made sense to a lot of people. I have come to realize that drumming was the foundation for this vision. According to researchers, repetitive, rhythmic sounds in a frequency range of 4 to 7 Hertz can bring on an altered state of consciousness. Shamanic practitioners say this type of drumming can induce a trance that can lead to journeying in the spirit world. To Native Americans, drumming has been historically and still is an important way of connecting to a higher realm where spirits can help us. My prayer on that rock came from my heart and this is what *A Course in Miracles* has this to say:

> *It is impossible that the prayer of the heart remain unanswered in the perception of the one who asks.*
>
> (CE)M-21.3

I asked for divine help sincerely. I was in a sacred place with all the energy of Native spirits ready to respond to a heartfelt plea for healing. Many thousands of people travel to Sedona each year seeking spiritual renewal. To these people, the vortexes here are powerful and very real. Some critics say all this is nonsense, but I am not one of them. I am a believer who is grateful for the holy encounter I experienced at the Enchantment.

CHAPTER 3

Deepening Through Understanding the Eternal Fixation

Riptide

I didn't think I could last much longer without taking a breath. I was tumbling, churning with no control over my body. I was underwater in a riptide with waves pulling at me like pit bulls with locked jaws. I was in full panic. *I am drowning.* Somehow the ocean spit me out. I lay in the sand gasping and crying.

This happened to me when I was about ten years old. My parents had a beach house in South Bethany, Delaware where we spent many lazy days on the beach playing in the water or later as teenagers, my sister and I working on our tans. This day my mother was sitting on a beach blanket, smoking a cigarette, sipping an adult beverage from a paper cup, and chatting up some other moms who summered at a leisurely pace.

After the ocean regurgitated me, it took me a few minutes to process what had happened. I looked at my mother some distance away thinking she must have seen me in distress but there she was sitting, sipping, and chatting away. No one had come to my rescue. *I almost died,* I thought. I needed someone to wrap their arms around me. To tell me I was safe. To tell me I was loved. Not to worry. Nothing to fear.

I staggered over to where my mother was sitting with her friends. My whole body was trembling as I slumped before her.

"Mom, did you see I was in trouble out there? I couldn't get above water to take a breath." I started to cry again. "I thought I was going to die."

All I wanted was for her to hug me and tell me everything would be OK.

But this is what she said with irritation in her voice, "You're fine." And with a push, "Now go away."

I was bereft. There was no comfort to be had. I walked away and sat quietly, hoping that at least the sun would warm me so I could stop shaking.

Many years later when I read about The Eternal Fixation (CE)T-5.IX, I began to understand. My longing for comfort, for love, and safety from my mother that day on the beach was a call for God. *"Fixation is the pull of God on Whom your mind is fixed because of the Holy Spirit's irrevocable set."*

My ten-year-old mind would not have been able to process this. All I knew was that a mother was supposed to love her children, comfort them, and keep them safe. My mother turned her back on me many times, not just the day I thought I would drown. So, I gave up that yearning and put on the armor of her "deal with it yourself/run it off" attitude as a way of protecting myself from her neglect.

Now through the lens of the Course, I realize my mother didn't do anything to me. I was responsible for making decisions about myself based on the things that happened in my life. When I judged negatively, I was mistaken.

But it turns out my yearning for protection, safety, and love is something we all want either consciously or unconsciously. In truth, it comes from only one source — God -not parents, friends, or life partners. In each of us, this yearning is old but not forgotten. It is called the eternal fixation...the pull for God that may have been pushed down into subconscious smoldering...but the pull for Him who loves us that has always been there and will be there until we find that place inside of us that feels His embrace.

You were eternally fixated on God in your creation, and the pull of this fixation is so strong that you will never overcome it. (CE) T-5.IX.9:2

CHAPTER 4

Deepening Through Holy Encounters

A COURSE IN MIRACLES encourages us to treat every meeting with anyone as a potentially holy encounter. When we accept this challenge, we see our brother or our sister as innocent children of God, wholly beautiful, and deserving of salvation. We accept and embrace our oneness. And we forgive him/her any false perceptions which we or they may have had.

The awareness of holy encounters came to me after my father's death. It was in the presence of a homeless man that I experienced the beauty of perfect love.

Homeless and Holy

What happened was not only surprising, but it was also shocking. My beloved father had died just two weeks before this unexpected event. At the time I was reeling from the joy of the shared death experience but steeped in grief at having to let my father go on to heaven. I missed him terribly.

I was walking down a sidewalk near my home when I became aware of what looked to me like a homeless man. He had stringy, dirty, long hair and tattered clothes. He looked dispirited shuffling along at a very slow walk with his head bent and looking downward as he neared me. In that moment everyone else around me faded and blurred. The scene before me was in sharp focus. The sad-looking homeless man had my full attention. Then something miraculous happened. His head came up in slow motion as he focused on me intently. His mouth, and indeed his whole face, changed into a brilliant radiant smile aimed only at me. He was beautiful beyond words!

As he walked on the smile slowly disappeared and the depressed homeless man slowly gazed back downward, and he journeyed on. I was so shocked! I felt like this man was my father even though he didn't look like him. I became frightened by this thought realizing it would seem crazy to go up to this man and hug him and tell him how much I loved him. I had at first perceived this man through my ego—he was dirty and homeless. But with his amazing smile, he showed me who he really was — a beautiful, holy child of God. It may be that the beauty of his smile reminded me of the love my father had for me. Perhaps it was my father's spirit within this man on the street. It doesn't really matter. What matters is the love that came through. It was pure and innocent and fills me with awe to this day as I recognize what holiness looks like and feels like—a gift from God.

I have learned that sometimes a holy encounter involves more than just one other person. I have also learned that the unexpected can deliver gifts well beyond worldly things.

No Words

I wanted to give Liz a luxury cruise, a spa vacation, or a few nights at a high-end hotel. She wanted none of those. All she wanted was isolation, quiet, and rest.

Liz had taken care of our beloved mother-in-law when Mary was dying of brain cancer. Then when Mary passed, she had to deal with Mary's husband whose poor judgement and at times mean-spiritedness made it even harder for Liz to maintain her poise and her patience. But she had.

My then-husband and I were so grateful for Liz's devotion to Mary and her generosity towards Mary's husband. We wanted to say thank you in a big way. But "big" to Liz was "No frills, please." So, I put a five-day stay at a monastery on our list.

It made perfect sense that she chose the religious retreat center. Liz had been a Catholic spiritual director for many years. She tended to others needs so often and now she needed some tender loving care herself. The New Camaldoli Hermitage at Big Sur, California offered everything Liz needed. Solitude. She would be staying in a cottage all by herself with no one nearby. Silence. Talking was not allowed anywhere on the grounds except the bookstore and then only to register or check out. The views were spectacular.

I decided to book a room for myself at the monastery for 3 days out of curiosity but also respect for the deep spirituality

Liz and my mother-in-law shared. They often told me of the benefits they gained from attending silent retreats. I had never been silent a day in my life. The idea of a strict no-talking rule scared me.

The Catholic retreat center was located high on a mountainside overlooking the Pacific Ocean. As Liz and I drove to the monastery, hugging the scenic and rugged California coastline, I spoke to her of my fear.

"I don't know what to expect out of being silent. Sounds lonely and a little frightening."

"The best thing," Liz said, "is to have no expectations. Just surrender to the stillness and answers will come."

I was willing but didn't have a lot of practice. I had chosen to come to this silent retreat with the hope I would deepen spiritually in a new way. Now I just had to have faith that those "answers" Liz talked about would come.

My first brush with those answers began as I checked myself in at the bookstore. I had flown to Texas about a month before my dear mother-in-law passed to see her one more time. Mary had wanted me to pick some belonging of hers to remember her by—something that would have special meaning for both of us. I asked her if she had a St. Francis statue knowing how deeply she cared about the Catholic saints but also knowing how much I loved animals. St. Francis loved the animals too and the natural environment. Mary didn't have a St. Francis statue but insisted we go shopping to find the perfect one. We looked but I didn't see any that spoke to my heart—too small, too big, wrong facial expression, etc. Mary told me to keep looking after I returned home and that when I found just the right one it would come from her heart as well.

I hadn't looked. Shopping didn't seem like the right thing to do when the grief of losing her weighed heavily on my mind. Now as I looked around the monastery bookstore after we arrived, my gaze settled on a surprise. There on the top shelf, tucked into a corner, was the most beautiful St. Francis statue I had ever seen. But it was expensive. Too expensive I thought. Disappointed, I turned my back on it and, instead, settled into my spartan room with the gorgeous ocean view.

Now what? I had no plan and that made me anxious. I didn't know what, if anything, to do but try and empty my mind and snuggle up to the silence. I went for a walk down the winding road that led to the highway far below. There were benches at various places along the way — a chance, I thought, to sit and drink in the beauty along with the silence. But every time I sat down, my mind was flooded with the image of that lovely St. Francis statue. It was like a tune you just can't get out of your mind. Just a distraction. An annoyance to divert my attention from sinking into silence.

And then it hit me. This was one of those answers Liz said would come. Mary had told me when I found the perfect St. Francis it would come from her heart. I had found the perfect St. Francis. Suddenly the expensive part was of no importance. I walked back up the road with conviction and purpose. The statue was waiting for me at the bookstore. Now with great joy, I bought it and placed it on the little desk in my room. Just looking at the beautiful face and peaceful expression on the statue, I could feel the convergence. Mary's love for me. She had said this gift would come from her heart.

My love for Mary. And St. Francis signifying a love for animals. It had come together perfectly. I knew I would be reminded of my love for Mary every time I looked at my beautiful St. Francis.

I was faithful to the rule of silence at the retreat. My time there had already been eventful. On the third evening just as the sun was beginning to go down over the Pacific, I walked to a bench at one of the highest points on the cliff. To my happy surprise, Liz was sitting on the bench but there was enough room for the two of us, so I joined her. We smiled at one another but did not speak. I felt such a deep love for this woman who was more a sister than a sister-in-law. I hoped my feelings for her would flow out to her in the space between us on the bench.

Suddenly we both noticed something moving out from the woods below us. As it advanced towards us, we could see it was a beautiful reddish-brown fox. It kept on walking towards us getting closer and closer—now alarmingly close! *What is this wild thing doing?* I thought. *Is she going to attack us, bite us? Oh, Lord!*

Liz and I looked at each other with wide eyes, both of us still silent but not sure what to do. Should we run? Should we try to wave off the fox? Instead, we just watched her as she came right up to our feet, turned around, and sat on the ground between us facing the ocean.

The three of us stayed there, not moving, never flinching, all of us directing our attention to the beauty before us. The sun was just beginning to dip down to the horizon, sky and ocean blending into a mesmerizing image of blue and gold.

Spokes of intense light reached out to form a halo of radiant beams around the sun.

The fox and the two women shared an instant of exquisite beauty and connectedness. And when the sun finally disappeared on the horizon, the fox slowly rose and began the trek back down the hill to her den.

Liz and I looked at each other in utter amazement. *There's that convergence again*, I thought. My love for Liz, her love for me, and St. Francis' love for animals forming a perfect communion between the three of us — me, Liz, and the fox appreciating the beauty of the light from the setting sun. I imagine the messengers of God wanted us to share in this moment of silence and understanding that all of God's beings are but rays of the same light. Thank you, God, for Mary and Liz, the fox, and the sunset. We joined in a holy encounter—a moment of grace that will live in my memory forever.

I have also learned that a holy encounter can come in the middle of conflict. It can be one person extending their light who breaks through the strife.

A Shot at a Miracle

A distressed pharmacist found his day turned right side up when a vaccination patient offered a miracle. I arrived at my appointment five minutes early but had to wait another forty minutes to get my shot. The pharmacist was not having a good day, likely after a long string of not-good days. The workload was bearing down on him after a long stretch of being short-handed. Now he had 6 people waiting for vaccinations and another line of people waiting for their prescriptions. It was going to be a long frustrating day. To make matters worse, one of the vaccination patients told him another pharmacy was sending patients to his store because they too were overworked and understaffed.

"This is just wrong! They can't be doing this to me making my life so much harder," exclaimed the pharmacist in dismay. He continued filling out his paperwork and preparing the vaccinations, but he was clearly upset. His eyes were downcast, and he muttered at patients as they showed up at his window. Without looking at them he pushed a clipboard and paper in their direction and told them to fill out the form.

I continued to wait quietly. I didn't want to add to the pharmacist's troubles so I asked the Holy Spirit, "How can I help?" I didn't know what to say but I trusted some helpful words would come. Finally, the pharmacist called my name to come into a small room and get my shot.

When I came through the door I said, "I bring you peace." I don't know why I said that. It just came out.

The pharmacist responded, "I wish."

I said, "No really. I bring you peace. Just take a deep breath." We both did just that. I said, "I hope you can let go of this stress when you go home."

He said, "Other people are making my job harder and harder. At the corporate level they don't want me to go home. They don't even want me to take a day off. How am I supposed to lose this stress if I never get a break? They tell people they can get four vaccinations at once. That's not safe, but it's my liability they are messing with not their own. I will only give one or two vaccinations per person. Do you think corporate cares about you?"

I listened intently. "I know they don't care about me. But I care about you. You are doing such a tremendous public service giving these shots and getting people the medicines they need."

He said, "Lately I've been questioning my career choice since most people just don't care about what I do."

"Well, I care, and I applaud you for all that you are doing."

"Thank you," he said quietly.

I got my vaccination—barely felt the shot. "Blessings on the rest of your day," I offered as I left.

As I walked out, I heard the next patient say to the pharmacist with much concern in his voice, "How are you feeling?"

He said in a gentle, upbeat voice, "I'm better now."

Miracles are miracles, not some small, some big. And how do you know if you've had one? You find peace. And the ripple extends. His peace was my peace. And the people waiting in line...and who knows how many after them. Holy encounters can extend to many others. Thank you, God, for the gift of a miracle this day.

Holy encounters can be overlooked but when you remember the potential for every encounter to be holy the rewards are stunning.

Beauty and the Barista

I was excited to meet a new friend at a local coffee shop. She's an Episcopal priest so I thought what might unfold between us would be holy. When I came into the café, I noticed she was already seated with her coffee in front of her. I waved and pointed to the counter. I would go order my drink and then join her.

A young man asked me what I would like to order. I looked the menu over and said, "I'll have a Chai Tea Latte."

While he busied himself making my drink, I slipped my hand into my purse to pull out my wallet. My wallet was not there! *Oh no,* I thought, *I must have left my wallet at home.*

"I'm so sorry but I can't have the Chai Tea or anything for that matter," I told the young man. "I must have left my wallet at home. I can't pay."

He looked up at me and smiled, "I want you to have this drink. Please don't go home and look for your wallet or come back in a few days to pay. I want to gift you this drink."

As he was talking, I searched my purse again and put my hand on a small card I carried with me to remind me to treat any encounter as potentially holy. *Was this a holy encounter unfolding before me?* When I looked up at him, I thought, *why did I not notice how beautiful this man is?*

That's when I knew this was indeed a holy encounter. He appeared incredibly beautiful before me. He was beaming at me with his lovely pure and innocent open heart.

"Thank you so much! You are incredibly generous," I said as I once again reached into my purse to touch the holy encounter card but now, I was feeling something else. I pulled it out from the slot in the small purse. It was a twenty-dollar bill I had forgotten all about.

I showed it to the beautiful barista and said, "Now I can pay you!"

"I wish you hadn't done that," he said with a smile. "I really wanted to give you a gift."

"You already have," I said with a smile as big as his own.

Many of us have regrets when we look over our lives. Whenever I thought of my regrets the same one kept coming up again and again. I carried something that happened in elementary school with me through most of my life. I was ashamed about what had happened and now it was too late to make it right. Or maybe not.

Never Too Late

Trudy cooty. That's what they called her—the group of bullies in my sixth-grade class. She was just twelve years old, thin as a waif, shy as could be. She wore what we called coke-bottle eyeglasses, thick and odd looking especially on a child. That made her look different from others in our class. She never spoke up for herself, but she bravely showed up each day of school. And each day the taunting continued. "Trudy cooty, Trudy cooty." "Don't dare touch her or you'll have cooties all over!"

The bullies were unrelenting on the playground. "Stay away from her! Trudy cooty smells," and they would hold their noses and point at poor Trudy. She was never chosen to play a group game but left for last when team captains made their selections. "Aw, you're stuck with Trudy cooty," they would say when Trudy stood there alone, the last one to join a team. Trudy's eyes were often downcast, but I never saw her cry.

You would think the teacher would have intervened. She never did even though the mistreatment happened both on the playground and in the classroom. I cringed every time they called Trudy names. But I never stood up for her. I knew the bullying was very wrong but still, I remained silent. I don't know why. Perhaps I was afraid the bullies would turn on me.

Many times, during the sixty-plus years since I knew Trudy, I have reflected on this failing of mine and always with regret and a measure of shame.

Now all these years later a miracle has been delivered. Here's how it unfolded: A dear Course in Miracles friend sent me a message on Facebook. She said, "This is you" and below was a lovely drawing of a sweet young girl with flowers in her hair and all around. When I clicked on the picture, sentences rolled out, animated over the image. They read:

> "She was BEAUTIFUL. But not like those girls in the magazines. She was beautiful for the way she thought. She was beautiful for the sparkle in her eyes when she talked about something she loved. She was

beautiful for her ability to make other people smile even if she was sad. No, she wasn't beautiful for something as temporary as her looks. She was beautiful deep down to her soul. She is beautiful."

And the sentences continued:

"Every woman deserves to be reminded of this simple message — that she's beautiful for who she is, not just her looks. That she's special to you in her own way. A few words can change someone's whole day, please pass this on to the beautiful women in your life. You know who they are... Thank you!"

Tears welled up in my eyes when this lovely animation ended. I thought of my dear friend and felt such love for her and gratitude that she would send me this tender message. I glanced over to the left of my messenger screen and saw a new entry just above my friend's. It was from Trudy! When I saw her name my shame and regret came back all at once. I thought after these many years she had found me on Facebook to finally tell me what a schmuck I had been in sixth grade. But instead, the message read "Hi. It's Trudy. We went to elementary school together. I have always remembered your kindness." WHAT? Did she say KINDNESS? Yes, she said she remembered my kindness...her entire life.

I sat there and cried. I had not remembered kindness, but she had. Trudy healed me with this one message. I looked at the date it was sent. It was sent a year ago. I had not seen it until this very moment my ACIM friend delivered her heartfelt message... "She is beautiful." Suddenly I knew how to make this healing complete. I wrote back to Trudy and told her how sorry I was to have not stood up for her when the bullies delivered their hateful taunts. I asked for her forgiveness and sent her the animated video my ACIM friend had sent to me, remembering the invitation to share it. "A few words can change someone's whole day. Please pass this on to the beautiful women in your life."

What if a few words can change not just a whole day but a whole lifetime! Trudy changed mine instantly with this holy encounter. Maybe now she can feel the love she always deserved. It's never too late.

CHAPTER 5

Deepening Through Divine Guidance

URING my years as a professional journalist, I was often struck by how often I got answers to some dilemma or other while I was asleep at night. These were during my years of spiritual laziness. If I had a problem with a story I was working on or pondered what to do about an editing issue in a documentary, I would think about it before I went to bed. Much to my astonishment a solution would be there waiting for me when I woke up in the morning. Maybe my mind dreamed about the problem and solved it on my own without realizing it. After my shared death experience when my belief in God was rock-solid, I began to understand that we all have access to divine guidance. Answers can come from outside our worldly consciousness, but we must still our crazy-busy minds to hear it. I have come to trust this as the truth because of personal experiences.

Let It Be

I was miserable. My high-powered, super-busy but rewarding career came to a screeching halt. I had become sick, barely able to get out of bed, wracked with pain, weak, and unable to eat.

I was diagnosed with a rare life-threatening primary immune disorder. There was no cure for this but there was a treatment — monthly intravenous infusions of immunoglobulins. It took a full year of these infusions for me to begin to get my life back, but I was still too sick to work. I was forced to retire from my job as a documentary producer. When I got enough energy to drive a car and do some simple chores like grocery shopping, I began to think about trying to find a greater purpose in my life. I joined an organization that paired caring adults to mentor children in foster care.

I was assigned to an eight-year-old girl named MJ and promised to spend up to eight hours a month giving her experiences she might not otherwise have. The idea was to provide emotional support, a steady commitment, and unconditional love. MJ and I have had many wonderful adventures over the years, everything from skipping rocks at the river, to horseback riding, to surfing lessons at the ocean. But in the second year of my friendship with MJ, her life became increasingly more challenging. She and her twin plus an older brother were moved from one foster home to another — four to five homes in one year. MJ was sometimes an hour away by car from me but sometimes as much as four hours away, but I always found time to spend with her. The children were traumatized with each move. On that fifth move, I became very angry with the system that would allow this to happen to children. I began to think about how I could harness all those years as a journalist into a force that could take that system down and rebuild it with something kinder and gentler for foster children.

I was filled with righteous indignation that I thought would provide the fuel to bring about real change. *I know how to push on things*, I thought. *I can do this.*

That weekend I attended a spiritual retreat with my anger in full force. I thought I was right to be furious and want to change things. This retreat, though, was about centering prayer, silence, and peace. I was not getting any of it. My anger was preventing me from feeling any peace.

Suddenly, I got a very strong message from what I believed was a divine source that I should lose the anger. I couldn't understand why. But every moment I resisted, I felt that message again "Lose the anger. Be patient. Find peace. Let it be." I didn't want to let it be. I wanted my anger to help bring change to the foster care system. By the end of the retreat, I finally surrendered the anger because the call to do so had been so persistent and so obviously not from me. I felt there must be a reason behind this divine guidance that I did not yet know. I decided to follow these messages, have faith, and be peaceful and patient.

The day after the retreat I was at my son's house when the director of the mentoring organization reached me on my cell phone. He said, "We finally have the new placement information on MJ and thought you would enjoy hearing where she is now. Take a guess where they have moved her."

My anger returned because I thought, *how could he think I would **enjoy** hearing about yet another wrenching move for this precious child?* So, I said the most unlikely place I could think of. "She must have been moved to my little country outpost in the foothills," I said with sarcasm dripping from my voice.

"Yes!" he said. "They moved her to a family just down the street from you!"

My heart leapt. Now I knew the reason for the divine message to wait patiently without anger. Instead of two hours from me, MJ would now be 2 minutes from me.

MJ is a grown woman now and looking back I can see that the foster family near me provided her with a lot of love and stability for many years and I was there to help her thrive. Thank you, God, for helping me not interfere with a miracle that was underway. I didn't need to do anything. I just needed to let it be.

A Hike with God

I have this amazing woman friend who is still on television well into her senior years. She's making the rest of us proud. Of course, she looks great, but it is her competence as a meteorologist and her personal presence that continue to attract TV news managers and viewers. She and I became friends more than forty years ago when I accepted a job as a reporter for the local NBC affiliate. Back then she was the "weather girl". Today she is not only a meteorologist but accomplished in so many other areas: a master gardener, sports expert, marathon runner, dog rescuer, piano player, skier, and the list goes on.

Kristine and I both love the outdoors so instead of meeting for lunch, we made plans for a hike in an area we had never visited before. Hidden Falls Park is in the foothills near

Auburn, California. We met in the parking lot there and started our trek, talking and catching up with one another along the way. Kristine and I are aware of the self-control we put into our careers, making things happen, and forcing our goals to be realized. In more recent years, we have talked about letting go of that control to let God take the lead. But going with the flow takes practice and our desire to control was habitual. We both were working on this but found we reverted to our old ways all too often. Our hiking experience at Hidden Falls turned out to be an incredible lesson.

We began our walk at the trailhead which took us along a creek, then turned many times over wooden bridges but there was always a creek next to us. We walked and talked for an hour admiring the waterfalls along the way and the beautiful, lush foliage of the park. An hour out and an hour back. It was time to head back. Before we turned around, I told Kristine I thought the creek was flowing in a different direction than when we first started. How could that be? First flowing north and now flowing south. Neither of us accepted this clue that perhaps we were not where we thought we were. Kristine said she was sure she knew the way back.

"Just follow me!" my confident friend said.

An hour later we knew we had made a mistake because we were on an unfamiliar path. We tried retracing our steps only to become more confused. Kristine picked a different fork in the trail telling me, "I'm positive this is the way back to the trailhead."

Kristine is quite an experienced hiker, so I was happy to let her lead the way. We found the creek again and felt relieved to be on our way to the parking lot. By now we had been walking for three hours and a bit of fatigue was setting in. Half an hour later we reached a fork in the trail with several paths in front of us. We had no idea where we were because no such fork presented itself when we began our hike. My confident, competent friend reached her breaking point. Her lips quivered and tears started to flow.

"Sue, I can't believe I've gotten us so lost. I'm sorry. I'm looking at these paths and I don't have a clue which to take. Can you take over now?"

I looked at the paths and said, "I thought staying along the creek would lead us back, but it isn't. It's like we're in an alternate reality and I'm as lost as you."

"Well then just pick any path," she said with a tremble in her voice, "I'm done."

I was quiet for a few moments and then said, "There might be another way. The one thing we have not done is to ask God to help us. Would you be open to a prayer right now?"

"OK," she said, "We've tried this on our own and failed miserably."

We bowed our heads while I prayed out loud for God's help. "Kristine and I were so sure of our directions today and we were wrong every time. We are tired now and still as lost as we were three and a half hours ago. We are ready to give up control of this situation. God, will you please take over and lead us on the right path to the parking lot? We surrender to your love. With gratitude and with peace we will follow your directions. Amen."

There were three paths in our view, one along the creek

northward, one on the creek southward, and one in the middle leading away from the creek. I felt God was telling us to leave the creek behind. This was a big surprise since we were so convinced the creek would lead us back to the parking lot. I told Kristine I wasn't sure about this new path but felt we were being asked to have faith that God would help us. Kristine followed in silence. We were going away from the creek, the creek no longer guiding us. In about 10 minutes we reached the top of a hill and what we saw on the other side astonished us both. Another trail intersected and looked entirely familiar to us. And there was another creek! There were two creeks and we had been following the wrong one. We were overjoyed to find the creek that would lead us home. Our steps quickened. We smiled and laughed. When the parking lot came into view I said, "You realize we wouldn't be here right now without God's help. I do believe God answers every prayer and He came through for us today."

Kristine looked heavenward. "I am not always right about everything. But You are. Thank you, God, for this lesson in letting go."

Now a couple of years since our hike along the creek, Kristine and I both still slip into our controlling ways from time to time. But when we do, we are reminded of our Hidden Falls lesson. God is the better hiker. We follow His lead.

This quote from *A Course in Miracles* is so perfect:
You have very little trust in me as yet, but it will increase as you turn more and more often to me instead of your ego for guidance. The results will convince you increasingly that your choice in turning to me is the only sane

one you can make. (CE) T-4.VIII.10:1-2

The Trivial and the Traumatic

I have trusted God with the big issues in my life — questions like "What would love look like?" and being led to my childhood best friend, Bill, to join in a holy relationship. That was a big deal. And I knew that reconnection was divinely guided. But what of the little things that come along in life? Why bother asking for guidance on trivial things? Things like which grocery store to go to and buy cookie-baking ingredients?

I planned to get my eleven-year-old twin grandchildren to my house the week before Christmas to bake Christmas cookies. Molly and Megan are so busy with activities and school I don't get to see them as often as I would like so I was especially excited to have them come for the day during their Christmas break. The day before our bake-a-thon I decided to go to the grocery store to get all the fun stuff to put on top of the cookies, icing, sprinkles, chocolate chips, and whatever other fun things I could find for decorating our creations. In the car on the way to the store I thought, *Which Safeway grocery should I go to? The one in Cameron Park about fifteen minutes away or the one near Placerville. also fifteen minutes away?*

At that moment I realized I was trying to decide by myself. Perhaps I could use this situation to test the Course's direction to always ask for divine guidance even for the small things. In Cameo 6 of the CE edition of ACIM titled "Letting Him Take Charge of Minutiae", Jesus tells Helen Schucman (Helen received messages from Jesus which became *A Course in Miracles*) that if she turned over the trivial things to Him, he would save her time so she could give miracles.

So now in my car headed to one of two grocery stores, I changed my mind.

OK, Jesus, I thought. *I won't make this decision by myself. Forget Safeway. I don't know where to go. Where would you have me go?*

Go to Save Mart. This is the message that came through almost immediately.

What?! I never go to Save Mart. The few times I'd been there in the past I was not impressed with either quality or inventory in the store. If this was heavenly guidance it certainly had that element of the unexpected I had come to view as a marker for the divine. I didn't think Save Mart would have the variety of cookie-baking goodies I wanted. I reminded myself that this was a test of the decision-making principles in ACIM. I had asked for help in this bit of minutiae. Had I been answered?

OK, I'll go to Save Mart, but I may have to go to another store after that to get everything I want for our baking extravaganza.

I pulled into the parking lot of Save Mart, curious what I would find inside. I checked the signs above the aisles to find baking supplies and made my way past the flour and sugar to the baking chips. I found just the right brand of chocolate chips and placed them in my basket then saw butterscotch bits and put them in too. My eyes glanced further down the aisle and to my amazement, the cookie-making goodies just went on and on to the end of the entire row. Reese's Pieces, peppermint chips, Heath Bar chips, sprinkles of every color, white sugar stars, cookies and cream pieces, and more and more...

I could hardly believe my eyes. No grocery store I had ever been to devoted an entire aisle to cookie-making goodies. As I surveyed the amazing array of ingredients and sugary extras I began to laugh.

Go to Save Mart.

Thank you, Jesus. Your guidance was perfect. You saved me time so I could spend more of it with my precious grandchildren.

We made more than 100 cookies but more importantly, we made wonderful memories that will warm our hearts for many years to come.

Just days after this little bit of fun, something far more serious grabbed my attention. My beloved thirteen-year-old yellow Lab became sick. Mac had been his sweet, loving, happy, healthy self until now. He couldn't keep his food down. He was drinking an excessive amount of water and had to pee constantly. I took him to the vet who ran some tests. "He's got diabetes and probably some other things going on. We'll start him on a regimen of insulin injections and see how it goes," the vet said.

I gave Mac insulin shots for several days but did not see an improvement in his condition. The vet had cautioned me not to give the shot unless Mac had eaten because that could precipitate a real crisis. Three days into his treatment he stopped eating completely. I called the vet. "What do we do now?"

"You could take him for a more comprehensive test to see what else is going on with Mac. An MRI would give us a lot more information. Two clinics in your area offer this procedure, but it is expensive," the vet cautioned.

"I don't care about the money," I said. "I just want to see what can be done to help Mac."

I called both clinics. The first one said MRIs were done without appointments. There might be a long wait time. And the cost was $900. At the second clinic, I learned appointments were taken and the cost was $600.

My husband, Bill, was driving as we headed home from a brief errand that morning. I told him I thought I should ask for divine guidance. He agreed. My question was which of the two clinics should I take Mac to for this MRI? Then I thought, *isn't this just what you learned a few days ago with the grocery store dilemma?* I had put limits on the answer by asking which of the two Safeway stores I should go to.

In *A Course in Miracles*, Chapter 30, in Rules For Decision Making, Jesus tells us:

"The outlook starts with this: Today I will make no decision by myself." Then continues... "This is your major problem now. You still make up your mind and then decide to ask what you should do."

Now I was again putting limits on the answer. Which clinic should I take Mac to... this one or that one? But I wanted very badly to DO something. Was I ready for the answer if I let the question be more open-ended? *I want to let go and let God, but do I have the courage to release my judgments and trust the guidance of the Holy Spirit?*

"I am going to do it," I told my husband. "I am going to turn this matter over to Jesus."

I took a big, deep breath. "Jesus, what should I do about Mac?"

My divine guidance came through instantly. **Don't do anything. Don't go anywhere.**

This was what I was afraid of. I knew that to not do anything meant Mac would die.

When we arrived home, I could see that Mac's condition had worsened. Not only had he stopped eating even when we tried every yummy treat we could think of to get him to eat something, now he had stopped drinking water and his back legs were failing him. In a panic, I called our vet again. What she told me made me so sad, but I knew it was the truth. She told me even If I took him for an MRI, we would only put a name to these things that had gone terribly wrong. If we opted to try emergency measures to stabilize him, we would inevitably face this same crisis again in a matter of weeks.

"It might be time to let Mac go," she said.

It was time. God knew it. The vet knew it. And now with tears streaming down my face, I knew it.

We called a mobile vet service to come out and euthanize Mac at our home. The vet was so gentle with him and so compassionate towards us all. Dear, sweet Mac put his head in my lap as I stroked him and told him how much we loved him, how much we had been honored by his presence in our lives. The sun was shining on the deck, and it was warm. Mac was wrapped in a soft blanket on his bed. He left this realm ever so quietly. I am grateful for the peace he experienced. I hadn't rushed him to this clinic or that clinic. He hadn't been frightened by being in a strange place and having people he didn't know poke him and prod him. He was home with the people who loved him for 13 years.

Following divine guidance isn't always easy but I know God's plan is always better than mine.

CHAPTER 6

Deepening Through Less Judging

I AM ALWAYS surprised when my judgments about others are wrong, in some cases, spectacularly wrong. I used to think I was a good judge of people but after my brother died, I had to face the simple truth that judging others is not a helpful spiritual practice.

My Brother's Family

I like to imagine that in the two hours before his death, my brother's colorful, silent friends came to see him and pay their respects. A school of Sergeant Majors with their distinctive horizontal black stripes would have swooped in close to his mask, then suddenly flitted backwards in a kind of ceremonial salute. Jon would have spotted the shy barracuda friend he always looked for, peeking around the corner of a knobby coral outcropping. He would have sent her a mental greeting, "Hi, Shirley!" A long, slender Trumpetfish would have poked its familiar large head out through a tunnel in a crystalline coral cave to herald my brother's presence. He loved these fish. They were family.

He had snorkeled along this coral reef just offshore from his Florida condo for thirty years. But on this day, all that experience meant nothing. My sister and I will never know what really happened. We know from autopsy reports that he didn't have a heart attack or a stroke. "... *a healthy, 52-year-old male... death by accidental drowning,*" the report read. It might have been a kind of "perfect storm" disaster. We know from witnesses my brother had been in the water for two hours. That's a long time. He was tired. Leg cramps are a possibility. People in the area noted some rip tides that morning. Life is fragile, and living is dangerous.

My heart broke when my sister called to tell me Jon was dead. A crueler blow came later when I learned my brother had called out for help. No one came. At least not in time. There were no lifeguards on this stretch of beach, and on a steamy Fort Lauderdale day in late June, only a scattering of tourists here and there. We were told a couple from Canada called 911, but no one who watched my brother shout and then sink, jumped in the water to help. When paramedics arrived, it was too late. My brother Jon died all alone. It seemed to us that Jon had lived with loneliness since his birth. He was born with a string of disabilities that didn't seem connected then, but fifty years later, doctors know a lot more about autism. His language skills were poor and his speech difficult to understand. He was tall and thin with an awkward Charlie Chaplin-like gait. Human touch was jarring, not soothing.

He lived with my parents until they died, Mother first then my father ten years later. In his will, Dad left the ocean-front condominium to Jon. I remember my brother asking me to look over his income and expenses. He was so scared without my father's guidance. "Do you think I can live on my own?" I told him I thought he could do it. "Margie and I will help you if you get into trouble." But my reassuring words belied my worry. I lived so far away in California. My sister was a little closer in Georgia. Jon was high functioning, but now he didn't have much of a safety net.

Before I returned to my home after my father's death, I helped Jon with some routine chores. It never occurred to me that grocery shopping together would be a major event in his life. As we were pushing our loaded shopping cart back out to the car, my brother said, "So this must be what it's like to be married...to do things together." I wanted to cry. My loner brother never had a prospective life partner, and I knew he never would. I was desperately sad he had missed so much in life—friends, a family of his own, children. I wanted him to at least know he had people who cared. "Jon, Margie, and I love you very much."

It was always hard for him to look people in the eye, so he stared at the cereal boxes in the cart. "Yes, and I love you too. Most people think I'm stupid and that's OK with me. They just don't understand."

I ached for him. Few people knew that he was brilliant in some areas, particularly military history. He could recite battle names, dates, officers, and strategies for military conflicts from ancient to modern times. He remembered the tiny details of ordinary events. In his letters to me, he wrote pages of details on his solitary travels through Florida. Sometimes it was how many steps it took to get to the car from a restaurant or the color, feel and price of the shirts he loved to buy. "Stopped at the outlet stores and picked up six more shirts. A green, a purple, bright yellow, red, white with blue stripes, and brown with a white stripe. The green one was the softest. It was $16.99..." and on and on he would go about the shirts. "I know I buy too many, but I just can't resist." But he lived within his means and managed his life responsibly, all by himself, for a decade after my father's passing.

Now my brother was gone. Without a word, my sister's embrace at the airport unleashed shared memories that brought us both to tears. Our brother's lonely life had ended with a tragedy that only underscored his isolation—no friend to join him snorkeling, not even a bystander to help when he was in trouble. We stopped at an Episcopal church near Jon's home before we drove to his apartment to begin the task of settling his estate. We decided we wanted to hold a memorial service for Jon even if we were the only two in attendance. My brother held a job with Broward County Water and Wastewater Services as a maintenance worker for nearly 28 years. We sent his supervisor an email about the memorial service. There were no others to notify.

Our first look inside my brother's condominium brought shock. Along the wall in the living room were stacks and stacks of hardcover books. We found more in every room. At the final count, there were more than a thousand books, mostly history and famous military leaders. Hundreds of other boxes were stacked in the rooms and closets, all filled with tiny military figures — the total well into the tens of thousands. He had a hat collection of beautiful English derbies, and then there were the shirts. Row after row, shelf upon shelf of polo shirts — the ones he told me he couldn't resist. There was almost no furniture in the apartment, just boxes and books, and clothes. At first glance, it looked like chaos reigned. But the shirts had been carefully laundered, folded, and arranged according to color or pattern. The boxes of military figures were each labeled according to country, conflict, and date, and arranged chronologically. Margie and I began to understand. The collections and the careful categorizing and labeling were my brother's way of adding structure and meaning to his life. He reveled in the small details and clung to them to make his way in a world that otherwise probably didn't make much sense to him. Clearing away his things brought us new insights and even more sadness that the world had so little understood this gentle soul. With stories of greed, selfishness, hatred, and disrespect grabbing today's headlines, my brother was an unsung gentleman, full of integrity—dependable, unflaggingly kind, utterly honest, and respectful. But the world did not notice or care about his life or his death.

My sister and I didn't hurry to get to the memorial service on time. There would just be the two of us, and perhaps my brother's supervisor. I was stunned when I walked into the church sanctuary. At least fifty people, maybe more, were taking their seats near the front of the chapel. My sister and I were confused and curious at the same time. *Who were these people? Where did our lonely brother meet them?*

The priest said, "I had a short service planned for Jon's two sisters but now it seems with so many people here it might be more meaningful to hear from them."

The people in the pews began to raise their hands. A wondrous, yes miraculous, transformation began to unfold for me and my sister. Could our view of our brother have been wrong? All our lives we had worried about Jon, pitied him, saw him as lacking a so-called normal life. Now these people had come here out of their great need to share what they knew about Jon. The stories poured out from their hearts.

All of them worked with my brother — every one of them — from fellow maintenance workers to construction workers, secretaries, and supervisors. One man stood, looked at Jon's sisters, tugged on his cap and said to us, "I worked side by side with JP for many years. You know, he never missed a day of work. Had to be forced to take time off. He loved the stray cats around the job sites and fed them regularly, talked to them, patted them even. There was one really scruffy one nobody liked but Jon. When your brother took off for a week or two of vacation, this cat just disappeared. We thought he was gone for good. But he showed up the morning Jon came back… every time."

A big, muscular man with several days of stubble on his handsome face offered another story. "Your brother loved the big machines, especially my dozer. I just got the biggest kick out of his reaction when he got assigned to help me — like a little kid, so excited. My boss told me Jon was a great assistant but warned me to be careful with instructions. Keep it plain and simple. Well, it was getting dark, and I had given him a list of instructions to turn off a piece of equipment — twist this knob, check that flange, flip this switch. I took out my flashlight and handed it to him. 'When you're done shuttin' it down, Jon, hit me with the light.'" It took me a few seconds, but from Jon's horrified look, I knew — holy crap! "No, no. Don't HIT me with the light. Just shine the light on me." The room full of people who had been dabbing at their eyes now dissolved into laughter.

Person after person stood and shared a lovely story about my brother's kindness, his honesty, and his surprising brilliance. "We had a pool going with the New York Times crossword puzzles," another man said. "Nobody knew it — guess they will now — but I cheated on occasion. If I got stuck on a word, I would go find Jon and give him the puzzle clue. Took him maybe seconds to give me the right answer. Wouldn't ever enter the pool himself, but we challenged him one time with a stopwatch. He got the whole New York Times puzzle done in under twenty minutes. He was amazing!"

I stood and addressed the group, emotion choking my voice. "My sister and I spent a lifetime worrying about our brother, feeling so sad he had no family close by and no friends. Today I realize you were his family. You were the ones who loved him, supported him, and made him feel he belonged. These words are not enough, but thank you for looking beyond his disabilities, and for bringing his sisters from terrible sadness to great joy in one simple and surprising memorial service."

A Course in Miracles reminds me in the workbook that *"I could see peace instead of this. I can replace my feelings of depression, anxiety, or worry (or my thoughts about this situation or personality) with peace."*
(CE) W-34.5:4

I keep one of Jon's beautiful English derby hats on my desk and a few of his military figures scattered here and there in my house. I want to always remember how he touched my life and how wrong my assumptions were about his loneliness. His life was far from empty or sad. My ability to see my brother in a different way allowed me to move from depression and worry to peace.

On that last day, out beyond the surf, I imagine he felt comforted by the embrace of the seawater and the silence of the creatures he had come to love. I knew about that family, but I didn't know about the other one—the human friends who looked beyond his differentness to let Jon's good heart touch their own. A month after his death, Jon's supervisor sent us a photograph from the county maintenance yard. It was a picture of a new street sign. The maintenance workers installed it on a road they pass every day. It reads, "Jon Pearson Way". The world may not remember my brother, but his family always will.

CHAPTER 7

Deepening Through Healing

MEDICAL DOCTOR and best-selling author Bernie Siegel popularized the concept of the mind/body connection with his best-selling book *Love, Medicine, and Miracles*. Dr. Siegel presented strong evidence the mind has tremendous power in fighting illness. Christian Scientists believe that illness is illusory and calls for spiritual renewal to heal rather than medicinal treatments. *A Course in Miracles* holds that sickness originates in the mind but that a patient should avail himself of traditional medical treatment if he believes it will help in healing.

It's often hard to accept that sickness is something that comes from within us rather than something the world outside imposes on us. I have come to believe that our difficulty in believing our minds cause illness is often because the thoughts we have about sickness are subconscious. I confronted this possibility when I received a cancer diagnosis.

Breast Cancer Journey to Healing

He was an impish leprechaun who delighted in turning

bad news into good news. "Something just told me to go back and take another look." The radiologist smiled at me with a playful look, proud of the gift he had for finding small cancers other radiologists had overlooked. There was no guile in him, more like glee to deliver the news that the cancer he found was early and treatable. That's what he told me about finding my breast cancer. He was looking at the mammogram I had just gotten a few days before and he really didn't see anything suspicious... at first. But when that feeling came over him to look again, he saw a little something, maybe nothing at all. He put my last three annual mammograms up on his screen and that's when he knew he was right to take another look. There was something there in the newest image that wasn't there before.

I wasn't shocked when the biopsy that followed indicated invasive lobular carcinoma. Twelve years earlier I had been diagnosed with lobular carcinoma in situ in that same right breast. LCS is not considered an actual cancer but a sign of increased risk. I took an estrogen-blocking drug in those intervening years to try and lower my risk. I guess it worked for more than a decade but now I was dealing with the real thing. There are two kinds of breast cancer — ductal which accounts for about 90% of cases and lobular, the rarer 10%.

My breast cancer surgeon thought she could remove the cancer with a simple lumpectomy which conserves the breast, but she cautioned that lobular breast cancer doesn't present as a lump. It is threadlike and can send tendrils out in many directions. She also said it is the trickiest cancer to detect early because it doesn't show itself readily on mammograms. Even so I thought my radiologist might have saved me the tricky part because of that "feeling" he had to look again.

My confidence was shattered when my surgeon called me a week after the lumpectomy to share the pathology report. Although the sentinel lymph node she removed did not show any cancer cells, the lobular cancer was not totally excised from the breast. She removed a lot of the tendrils, but the margins were not clear. She told me the only way to get rid of it was a mastectomy and said I might want to consider having both breasts removed even though the left breast showed no sign of cancer. It took me a minute to absorb the idea I would lose a breast but, in my mind, this was the only option for beating cancer. I told my surgeon I would think about having both breasts removed.

I went back and forth on the double vs the single mastectomy. I asked for divine guidance. I wasn't sensing any messages. Then I spoke with my good friend Sue on the phone. I filled her in on what was happening and as always, she was very supportive. She understood the dilemma of keeping one breast intact but also the risk of cancer developing in that remaining breast. We ended that phone call with a virtual hug across the miles but within seconds she texted me back. "Hope you have your sense of humor intact. Here's the thing — I've never known a woman to pass up a 2fer deal!" I laughed. I also had this wonderful warmth close over me and a feeling of peace. Divine guidance comes in many ways, and this was mine, delivered playfully but powerfully by my dear friend. I would opt for the two-for-one deal. I called my surgeon and told her I wanted a double mastectomy because I didn't want to risk cancer showing up in the future in the left breast. I also knew that I wanted breast reconstruction, and the best result aesthetically would come from rebuilding both breasts at the same time.

My spiritually sensitive friend Maridel knew I wanted to explore the deeper issue of why I had developed breast cancer. It is my belief and hers that nothing happens outside of us, and that mind and body are closely connected. She said it often helps to come up with a word to associate with the situation. Since breasts have the job of expressing milk to nourish babies, Maridel thought I might try on the word "expressing" as a tool to get to the truth. I thought there might be something to this approach but didn't know how it fit with my personal story.

A week before the surgery was scheduled another friend of mine, Sharon, emailed me a link to a free online healing workshop. She had heard this healer speak and thought she was good. There were five 30-minute sessions offered, one each day Monday through Friday. Since it was free and the notion of healing appealed to me, I registered for the course. On day one I listened as the healer explained most of us have some early trauma in our lives that remains unresolved and can lead to illness. Her voice was mesmerizing as she asked her online participants to search their earliest memories from childhood particularly up to age seven.

Eight years before this healing series I had an extraordinary reading from a renowned astrologist. He shares his reading as a kind of life story and as he told me mine, he captured the essence of my journey perfectly except for one thing. He said I had a very deeply repressed memory from childhood. He didn't know what caused this but suggested sexual abuse could trigger something like this. I really didn't think I had been molested as a child and couldn't think of another trauma that might have happened to me.

Now sitting at my computer listening to the healer speak, I unearthed that trauma. When I was seven years old my younger sister, Nancy, became suddenly unresponsive. I remember going with my mother to take her to the doctor but illness to me meant maybe a bad cold or the flu. Two days after the doctor visit, Nancy lay on the sofa in the living room, very still and not responding to touch or voice. My mother was trying to get her to talk by asking what she had done at the park a few days before. Nancy remained silent. I didn't really understand what was going on at the time only that Nancy was not acting normally. I thought I could help ease my mother's mind by telling her what Nancy and I had done at the park, so I began to describe our outing. My mother raised her voice and said to me, "Stop talking! I do not want you to talk. I want Nancy to talk." I felt confused and upset my mother would shut me down this way, after all I was only trying to be helpful. An ambulance came to the house. My mother and father went with Nancy to the hospital. A short time later, two-year-old Nancy was dead. The pathology report would later reveal that Nancy died from spinal meningitis. Nancy had slipped into a coma at home and that, of course, was why she was not talking.

I didn't know anything about death, perhaps a bird or a cat had passed away but not an actual much-loved human being. When my mother and father got home from the hospital they sat down with my older sister, Margie, and me. I remember being shocked to see my father cry. My parents told us of Nancy's death and said she had gone to heaven to be with God. She was never coming back. And this is when I made a mistake. Seven-year-old Susan thought... *my mother told me not to talk but I talked and a short time later my sister was dead. If I just hadn't talked Nancy would be alive. I caused my sister to die.*

Now, any adult or even an older child would not have made this conclusion. Young Susan concluded that she could not talk ever again and risk anyone else dying. And herein lies the repressed memory. I believed I had caused my sister's death, so I stopped talking altogether. It was too dangerous, and I was a bad girl for having this terrifying power. I didn't speak for an entire year. Expression was risky. My parents worried about me. I do remember them talking about taking me to a psychiatrist, but I don't remember if they did. And I hadn't remembered anything about my mistaken judgment until that first session with the online healer.

I felt a little dizzy and off balance when I told my husband of this repressed memory. I felt as though I had been hypnotized by the healer's voice. This must have been why I could delve so deeply into my psyche to uncover the repressed memory the astrologer had told me about almost a decade before.

The next day of the healing workshop the healer gently suggested we focus on any childhood trauma we had mined the day before. She wanted us to re-live it from the point of view of an observer. I was reluctant to revisit the day my sister,

Nancy, died. The grief from this event had gripped my entire family for most of our lives. But with the healer's compassionate urging, I went back there in my mind. I saw Nancy motionless on the sofa. I saw my mother kneeling beside her on the floor, distraught that her youngest daughter was gravely ill. I saw myself next to my mother, thoroughly confused and desperate to make some sense of this scene. My little sister and I had been running and laughing with abandon just a few days before at a local park.

Now as I replayed this memory, my throat began to tighten, my eyes welled with tears, my stomach in knots. I remembered the sheer terror of feeling I was responsible for my sister's death. I silenced myself so no one else would die from this awful power I had unwittingly released. It was only a mistaken belief! I had repressed this memory for some sixty years because the pain of this belief was too difficult to bear. Now as I confronted the truth that seven-year-old Sue had held herself a prisoner of a mistaken belief I doubled over in real physical pain. That subconscious belief colored my entire life causing me to feel unworthy and not loveable. I barely noticed when the online healer closed off the healing session with her loving words. I raced to the bathroom and threw up violently repeatedly. Diarrhea gripped me as well until from top to bottom there was nothing more to purge. I felt terrible. If this was healing, then who needed it?

At the final healing session, the healer asked us to see ourselves as young children who suffered trauma. She told me—the older, wiser Sue—to sit next to that seven-year-old Sue and put my arm around her as a friend. To ask the young Sue to tell me again what had happened. This time young Sue told older Sue, "I made a big mistake. I thought I killed my sister, but I had nothing to do with it. I wasted a lot of time feeling guilty and ashamed." The healer told me to ask young Sue what she needed now. The answer brought a flood of tears again. Young Sue said, "I need to be forgiven for my mistaken belief." Older, wiser Sue said through her tears, "I forgive you." As I sobbed, I turned my attention to God and said, "OK, I unearthed the trauma, the repressed memory, and I have let it go but why now? I am facing a double mastectomy in just a few days and that's enough stress without piling on these painful memories and undoing the mistakes." I received God's answer immediately. And I know it was from God because His answers are always surprising, unexpected, something I wouldn't have thought of myself. And here it is: *This memory and the cancer are all connected. You have done the hard part now, excising that judgment you made that wasn't true. It's gone. Poof! It disappeared. You can think of the surgical team as the clean-up crew.*

My husband and I woke up early on the day of my surgery. I was no longer tormented by facing the trauma in my childhood. I felt unburdened. As we drove to the hospital, I felt comforted by God's message that I had "done the hard part". My surgery team would just "clean up the remnants" from the message I had sent myself all those years ago that *expression* was dangerous, even deadly. In other words, my negative, damning, terrifying opinion of myself set up a situation in my body to interfere with *expression*. Since breast lobules are the seat of expression for the making of milk, breast cancer would be a likely place for those unexpressed, repressed, sub-conscious messages to gather and wreak havoc. Should I blame myself for getting cancer? I believe not. Blame and guilt would only compound the original mistake. Forgiveness is what is needed to undo the mistake and move on with lov-ing, healing thoughts. This is but a beginning for me to under-stand the cause-and-effect relationship of negative, unloving, and repressed thoughts. As my husband navigated morning rush hour traffic on our way to the hospital, a digital sign on the south side of the freeway caught my eye. It read, "Worthy of every expression..."

Thank you, God, for this healing. I finally feel worthy of every expression.

Sometimes it is not an obvious illness that calls out for healing but the healing of some mental and emotional crisis. This was the case with my most challenging life event—the crumbling of a long marriage. In my darkest hour, God came to visit and showed me what heals all hurts—love.

My Dark Night of the Soul

With the barest pause, she gave me a look, but in that nanosecond of silence, a seed of doubt was planted. My girl-friend and I were having lunch, catching up with one another as we had regularly throughout our 40-year friendship. We had supported each other through boyfriend breakups, mar-riage breakdowns, and career upheavals in all that time. She knew many of the difficulties I faced in my long marriage, but I think we both felt my husband was at the very least a loyal partner.

"I think we've finally arrived at a place of acceptance. He has his activities and I have mine. It's OK with me when he says he likes to hike alone. I'm happy that he's found something he likes to do," I told her.

She stared at me for a fraction of a second. "Okay," she said.

The next morning my husband of 24 years told me he was going on an all-day hike in the mountains…alone. *OK.* Then he got on his treadmill for his usual one-hour workout. *Why?* Then he was smiling and getting ready to leave. *Too happy.* Then I looked at his shoes. Regular shoes. Not hiking boots. *Something is not right.*

When he left, I sat at my desk for a long time. That seed of doubt was beginning to grow. My husband always had an explanation for everything anytime I raised questions. Over all those years I had come to doubt myself and dismiss any feeling I had that things were amiss in my marriage. But not this day. I kept asking myself, "Do you want to know? Or do you not want to know." After quite a while I decided the truth was what I wanted even if the truth was going to lead to a crisis. God would help me through this.

I went to my husband's desk in our bedroom and sat down in front of his laptop. His emails might lead me to the truth. When I opened his "sent" files the truth was all there in email messages. He had betrayed me time and again over many years. Now as I faced the truth about my husband, I told myself I needed time to come up with a plan to confront him, but other subconscious forces took over. I woke him in the middle of the night and told him I knew what he had been doing. There followed hours of ugliness on his part and mine. I had never experienced a rage so deep within myself. Near morning I said I would go stay in the guest house on our property. I couldn't stand another minute of being in this bedroom I shared with a man I no longer knew.

The first night in the guest house I cried a little. The second night I wailed. The third night a guttural, deep, primitive sound spewed out of my mouth and emptied my soul. I was shaken to my core. The fourth night I told God that though I didn't feel His presence I knew He was somewhere. I said, "God, would you tell me if I am going to die from this pain? I am in such a dark place. And if I'm not going to die then could I just rest some? I'm not sleeping. I just can't escape this nightmare." And finally, "If you answer me, would you show me your light, so I know it's You."

I got in bed and put on headphones to listen to music. The song that played was The Dark Night of the Soul, by Loreena McKennitt. She had put to music what St. John of the Cross wrote from a Spanish prison cell back in the 16th century. As Loreena sang the lyrics, I absorbed the truth of St. John's poem, *The Dark Night of the Soul*. I began to feel that God would find me, not where I had made up a way to feel His presence, but where He truly was in the great "I Am". And I offered in return "Here I am Lord."

"*... Oh night thou was my guide*
Oh night more loving than the rising sun
Oh night that joined the lover

To the beloved one
Transforming each of them into the other..."

Miraculously, God met me where I did not expect to find Him. I had always thought God was somewhere outside, over there, beyond the clouds, up in heaven. But this night God revealed He was joined with me deep within my mind. He answered in my stillness because of the sincerity and intensity of my call to Him. I had not numbed myself with drugs or alcohol. I waited in the pain that felt like a prison with no escape. But God showed me the way out. It was within.

St. John had written of the same experience in his prison cell.

"...I abandoned and forgot myself,
Laying my face on my Beloved.
All things ceased; I went out from myself
Leaving my cares
forgotten among the lilies."

When the song ended, I was filled with God's true presence, not outside myself, but deep within. It's nearly impossible to describe in words what was being communicated but I could feel God telling me how spectacular I was, how awesome, a wholly innocent beautiful spirit. I felt His deep love and appreciation and gratitude for me. And I returned this love to Him. There we were together as One. The exchange was so playful and filled with joy. God did not acknowledge my pain. He knew that love is the great healer, and he gave me that gift. To acknowledge my pain would have only made my suffering worse. I needed to release it. This pain did not come from my husband, it came from my thoughts alone. No one had done anything to me. Betrayal and humiliation were just my thoughts, nothing more. I was the one who invited darkness to bring me pain. And the light God brought this night had shined away the darkness in this dark night of my soul.

God showed me my divine holiness. I fell in love with Him and fell in love with myself. Love completely displaced the darkness where fear had resided. In these moments I knew God had delivered an answer to one of my questions: I would not die. Love would show me the way to healing. I would be okay. Then the next answer: I slept, deeply, soundly, dreamlessly. I had no sense of time, day or night, just a deep rest. I had asked God for that too. What awakened me was the strongest, cleanest, purest light imaginable pouring through the slats of closed window blinds in my room. I awoke from the strength of this light. As I sat up in bed and thought about what this dark night had brought me to, I knew that my third request had been answered. *"...and would you show me your light so I will know it's You."* Thank you, God. I will get through whatever is ahead with Your love guiding the way.

My dark night transformed me. In the days ahead it was clear my husband could not let go of his behavior patterns. He told me to find a marriage counselor but refused to go with me. Since God had shown me how fully worthy I was, how could I stay with someone who still turned his back on love. We were worlds apart. When I regarded my marriage an ACIM quote came to mind:

> *A desert is a desert is a desert. You can do anything you want in it, but you cannot change it from what it is. It still lacks water, which is why it is a desert. The thing to do with a desert is to leave.* (CE) T-1.43.12

There was no sustenance in my marriage, in other words, no water in the desert. So, I left.

I got a divorce and moved to another community. God had demonstrated that His love healed all hurts. Now it was up to me to do the work He wants all of us to do in this journey we take on earth. I had to find a way to release all barriers to love and let go of any bitterness I held toward my former spouse. I realized that in carrying this burden of anger I was hurting myself. I needed a way to find compassion for him and for myself, after all, I was a partner in this play he and I created. Forgiveness can come instantly to some but for others, like me, it is a process. In a matter of months, I was able to release my anger and bitterness. The past was gone and holding on to the negative thoughts was keeping me in a prison of hate. I surrendered it. I gave up judging him. I forgave myself. The roles we had played were of this world, but I had experienced another where only truth abided. We are all children of God which means we are each worthy and innocent. We have not sinned. We have just made mistakes. He made his. I made my own.

Forgiveness is the key to happiness.
I would awaken from the dream that I
am mortal, fallible, and full of sin,
and know I am the perfect Son of God.
(CE) W:11.69.13

I was so happy when the little girl I mentored was moved by the foster care people to a family just a few minutes from my home. They were good people who had fostered many a child in a stable environment. My journey with MJ doesn't end here.

Quiet Vigil

She stands in the corner looking out on the road. This is the only spot in the field that isn't shaded by large, sheltering, beckoning trees. The sun is beating down on her tired body. Her haunches are hollow with skin stretched tight over hip bones that protrude. Her back is swayed. Her shoulders bony. Her head bowed. She stands and she waits.

"Have you noticed that skinny horse in the pasture along the road to your house?" My neighbor asked. She and I sometimes run into each other at the feed store and today she was concerned about this sad-looking horse standing in the blazing sun with its head hung down looking forlorn and neglected.

I know this horse. Our lives are intertwined. The story is very different than it appears. To be sure there is suffering but along the way, there is an invitation to trust in a higher power—a chance to experience the nearness of God. Shiloh and I both have been touched by grace, our paths connected by some divine guidance.

Spiritual growth is often difficult and this chapter in mine began when a health crisis sidelined me from a successful career as a journalist into early retirement. My husband said, "Just stay at home and play with your horses." And while that sounded appealing it also sounded a bit self-centered. An organization called Wonder Inc. offered a chance to make a difference, not in the world or even my community but in just one life—the life of a child in foster care.

And so, I became a mentor to MJ, eight years old, hair color of wheat, eyes that sparkled, and a personality that said "I can, and I will" again and again. It's a quality that the people in child protective services call resilience and MJ had it. Her enthusiasm won my heart. "When can we start having adventures?... Can you teach me anything?... I love to learn." I explained to MJ that I had to have three home visits before we could start going out doing things together. Each time I came over I brought what I thought were interesting craft projects for us to do in her home, things like cake decorating, scrapbooking, and beadwork. She dove into each project but didn't have much to say. Where had the earlier excitement gone?

"Is there anything on your mind, MJ?"

"Yes, there is. When can we get outta here and start having fun?"

"OK, next time, I promise, we get out of here and start having fun," I laughed.

I told her a bit about myself. "I have five children; one girl, four boys, and mostly they are grown and gone from home. In six months, my youngest boy will graduate from high school and leave for college." MJ threw back her head and turned to me, her long ponytail flicking from side to side. "Well, aren't you lucky to have me now!" I laughed at her spunkiness. Looking back, this was the moment I fell in love with her.

We went to plays, concerts, and the zoo, skipped rocks

at the river, hiked in the mountains, played with my dog, and when a neighbor offered to loan me her child-safe pony I gave her riding lessons. I knew from my long years of riding and caring for horses that these animals offered an extraordinary learning experience. In honing good equestrian skills, a lot of amazing life skills get formed and sharpened. Things like leadership, patience, responsibility, self-confidence and more. MJ was a little scared when she first got on Diamond but with slow and steady guidance from me, she was ready for her first horse show within eight months. We borrowed show clothes, and together we groomed Diamond until the pony gleamed. In the show arena, I had to let go of MJ—no more helping. She was on her own now. I leaned against the arena fence, drumming my fingers nervously on the top rail.

I must have held my breath the entire time because when the judge announced the results with MJ awarded first place, the air came rushing out of my lungs in one huge whooping shout of joy. The smile on MJ's face could have lit up the universe. I was helping her with what is all too often missing in the life of a foster child—the opportunity to thrive. The surprise was how much she gave me back. I felt energized and needed.

Suddenly MJ was at a crossroads. From her social workers, she learned she would either return to her biological mother, be put up for adoption or stay in foster care until she aged out of the system at eighteen. Every option seemed scary.

While the unknown was looming, the thing she was most concerned about was me. I had indeed filled the role Wonder Inc. had intended—to be a consistent presence, the one who followed through on promises and offered a fount of unconditional love. "I'm worried we won't be able to be together." The usually upbeat MJ was somber. I did my best to reassure her. "Honey, as far as I'm concerned, I'm with you for life. Even if you get tired of me someday, you'll have a hard time getting rid of me." I hoped she would smile but she didn't. It's hard to trust when trust has been broken. I knew I would hang in there no matter what, but MJ wasn't so sure.

In a matter of weeks, MJ's mother lost her parental rights so going home was not an option. Social workers looked to find a family who would adopt her. This precious child was moved three times. I saw MJ try her hardest to bond with new parents, accept different rules, adjust to new schools, find new friends, and just fit in. But every time she did these things, she was expected to do it all over again somewhere else. The people who study the effects of the foster care system on children say these kids experience more post-traumatic stress than war vets. I understand.

I stayed connected through each move even though the foster families lived many hours away. MJ told me she had high hopes in the second foster home. "The room they had fixed up for me was so pretty. I thought I could be happy there." When I visited after the third move and took her out to lunch, she was desperately unhappy. At the noisy café, she leaned in close and said, "I told myself to just hang on because I knew when you got here you would make everything alright. Get me back to the other family quick, OK?"

I choked back tears, "Oh, MJ. I don't have these magical powers. I can't make everything alright. The only thing I can do is be your friend and love you through all the good times and bad times. I will hug you when you are sad. I will listen when you need to talk, I will be your cheerleader for life. Someday you are going to have a life of your own design and it's going to be wonderful." Now we were two broken hearts. Hers because I wasn't the hero she wanted me to be. Mine because I had to take away that illusion. I cried most of the way home.

Later I made plans with a stable near MJ to bring our borrowed pony for day trips so she could continue her riding lessons. I began to map out a routine and dream up new adventures. I knew there were some problems in the new family and that MJ was not doing well in school. I thought the foster care people would give this patched-together family time to work everything out. I was wrong. The director of Wonder called. "Sorry to have to tell you this, but MJ has been moved yet again, and I don't have the new contact information. We'll just have to be patient." *What!? Be patient? Are you kidding?* I couldn't believe what I had just heard. Four moves in six months! Outrageous!

But she was moved to a family within minutes of my home. God winked. I am sure of it. I was deeply humbled.

MJ flourished in a stable family with a foster mom and dad who had good values and solid parenting skills. They, and I, were committed to helping MJ succeed in life. She did well in school and joined the ranks of preteens everywhere with girlfriends, sleepovers, and a lot of giggling.

After a few months, she and I went to visit a friend of mine who operated a horse rescue center nearby. My friend knew of my mentoring journey with MJ. She said, "If you are ready to adopt a horse, I have one I have been saving for just the perfect home. Would you like to meet Shiloh?"

And that is how Shiloh came to live in the front pasture at MJ's house. The horse had been badly neglected, starved, and left in a barren field to die. MJ took excellent care of her horse with plenty of good hay and clean water. Shiloh was groomed and stroked tenderly every day. MJ rode her on a nearby trail or bareback in the front field. Shiloh and MJ developed a strong bond. They both knew about betrayal and hardship.

The mare trotted across the field in the morning as MJ walked from her house to the bus stop. It wasn't far. In the corner where the fencing meets, the horse saw her best friend being taken away in a big, noisy, yellow box. She had no idea where. But she was willing to endure the searing heat of the sun to wait there for MJ. Shiloh trusted her quiet vigil would end when her friend returned in the afternoon. A passage from the Bible frames this scene, "In silence and in hope will be your strength." As MJ stepped from the bus and walked along the fence line to the house, the horse trotted from the corner to the other end of the pasture to follow her home. They both learned that love is worth waiting for.

Now it is my turn to wait because so much has changed. Many years have gone by since MJ and Shiloh were best friends. There were some rocky moments and some wonderful times. I felt in the beginning of this journey with her that the biggest gift I had to give was my unconditional love. I believed that love could influence the course of her life. For a lot of years that seemed to be true. Even when she had a baby at age 17, I gave up my own dreams for her future and accepted whatever direction she wanted her life to take. When she left foster care at age 18, I helped her move into an apartment. She was so happy to finally have a home of her own. She got a job at a sandwich shop and worked out arrangements for her infant daughter's care. The baby's dad and the grandmother were fully involved. MJ got promoted to a manager position and was so proud to be trusted with this bigger responsibility. I was proud of her too. I gave her money or took her shopping when she needed extra funds for baby items or to pay bills or deal with unexpected car repairs.

We met regularly to stay in touch but something in our relationship began to change. She started asking for money more frequently. Then she started not showing up for our get-togethers. There were big lags in our communication. She seemed to be pulling away from me but at the same time asking me for more money. I began to hear from some of her friends and family members that she might be using drugs. Her decision-making ability seemed compromised, yet she would stay in touch with me if she wanted money. I didn't want to be just MJ's bank or enabler. I wanted to be her friend and be truly helpful.

I didn't think I was being truly helpful in continuing to supply her with money. I told her I would not be giving her any more cash. She continued to ask, even beg, but I stood firm on the issue of money. If she was doing drugs, then I didn't want to help her down that dangerous path. I prayed for her. I offered to take her shopping and pay for whatever she needed.

She withdrew from me completely. I found out that she quit her job. Then I found out she had another baby.

I felt I had been a failure. I had extended so much love to MJ over the years. I thought it would help her heal from the trauma of her early years. But the love I gave then, and still offer her now, hasn't seemed to help her in this part of her life. I continue to text her with loving messages, but she does not respond. I realize I have more to do, but it is myself I must work on now. There is healing to be done. I must forgive myself for feeling like a failure. I must trust that my gift of love was received and that it awaits her acceptance. Like Shiloh the horse, I must hold my own quiet vigil because love is always worth waiting for.

CHAPTER 8

Deepening Through Gratitude for Our Beloved Pets

ACCORDING TO the National Institute for Health, 68% of U.S. households have a pet. Those of us who love our animal companions appreciate that they view us with unconditional love. What a comfort! NIH findings also report that pets may also "...decrease stress, improve heart health, and even help children with emotional and social skills."

I have come to believe that the love they extend to us can also protect us from danger. I know this because of two such guardian angels in my life — a dog named Nick and a cat named Addie. A horse named Bella confirmed to me that heaven has a place for animals.

Tribute To a Hero

Together we each wrote goodbye letters and put them inside a grave marker that read "Beloved Friend". It's difficult enough to bid a final farewell to a loyal pet but when it's a guardian angel who has transformed lives, the tears feel more like torrents of grief mixed equally with gratitude. Our friend

MJ's note read, "We will love you and miss you forever." My granddaughter's note read, "We will never forget what you did for so many, especially me. Thank you." My letter was a copy of a story I wrote that was published in the local newspaper when our dog, Nick, first became a hero many years ago.

The Sacramento Bee piece titled the story "Just in The Nick of Time". It began like this:

"When life is moving very fast, but everything seems to be in slow motion, you can be sure nothing good is happening. The events speed up the action. The fear slows it down.

Weeks later in my mind, I see Nick and Adam over and over again. Perhaps so I'll never forget. I know I never will.

Nick is our dog, a yellow lab, still a puppy really — not yet two years old. Adam is the twelve-year-old friend of my son, Evan. What began on June 20 as an adventure on a bright, warm, sunny day by a mountain stream was to take a sudden dark turn."

What followed in the story seemed like a disaster, but it was really a miracle. It was the day before the first day of summer and the river beckoned. I told the boys they could only go wading and only in one shallow section of the river upstream and only if I went with them. It was that compelling an idea even if Mom had to come along so off we all went including Nick the dog to sample the first of summer's refreshment. We arrived at the spot I had dubbed "safe" and the boys proceeded to roll up the pant legs of their jeans. Nick splashed along the shore enjoying the cold water rushing by but not in a hurry to join the strong currents bent on finding a more tranquil home in the valley. I had taken Nick's leash off to let him play and I stood on the shore filling what I thought was the role of responsible parent watching the boys and the dog.

Life couldn't be better. Everyone was having one of those moments of simple pleasure we look back on years later to realize was in fact a treasured memory—one of the reasons life is so sweet. Adam is joking with Evan —a twelve year old challenge." Go all the way under, Evan, I dare you!" Evan is laughing and hesitating.

Suddenly it is Adam who is all the way under. He slips on the rocks. He is immediately swept into the unforgiving current. In those split seconds which have now become vivid snapshots of terror engraved in those parts of my brain reserved for life and death reactions, I remember thinking I was watching a tragedy unfold. I ran to the edge of the water and yelled for Adam to catch the dog leash I was throwing. I missed. He missed. He went underwater again and looked up at me. Eyes wild with fear seemed to plead, "Help me!"

I saw paramedics arriving after Evan had run back to the cabin to get help from his dad. I saw them pull Adam's lifeless body from the chilly water and work on him for an hour. I saw Evan sobbing on the shore forever changed. I called Adam's parents.

There would be no birthday party next Saturday. Instead, a funeral. I could never forgive myself for letting the boys go in the water. Adam's loss would weigh us all down for the rest of our lives. None of us would love the little cabin in the mountains again. This landscape would be a tangle of pain, and grief, and sorrow.

But none of this happened. In those split seconds of heightened awareness, I saw a blur of yellow fur flash by. It was Nick. He jumped in the water and swam to Adam as the current thrust the boy away. I saw Adam grab a handful of fur and skin like his life depended on it. It did. Nick never hesitated. He swam to shore pulling Adam with him. Adam climbed out of the water shaken and shouting at the same time "Nick, I love you!" Nick shook himself off and casually walked over to me and sat down.

Thank you, God. Thank you, Nick — in the Nick of time to save us from a lifetime of grief, deep sorrow, and regret."

My hero dog died just a few months ago of old age. I held him in my arms as I said goodbye. He lived to be thirteen and not only was it a good life for him in the country with ten acres to explore and rule, but it was also a life full of more heroic deeds. He had that courage in his DNA. In the years after he saved Adam's life he was always on duty for more acts of courage on our behalf. A neighbor and her two-year-old toddler ventured near my thoroughbred horse, who, seeing strangers approach, had a fit of hysteria; bucking, rearing, and stampeding around his paddock. I saw it from afar. Nick sprinted to the paddock and got between the two-year old and the out-of-control horse, gently nudging the boy out of harm's way. Then there was the time another neighbor was visiting me at the barn when a German Shepherd across the way charged her. I yelled at Nick, "Get him!" and Nick went after the dog, and with a fury pushed him into submission, forcing him to run back home with his tail between his legs. Like Adam, my neighbor said, "I love you, Nick!" when the danger was past.

He was most dramatically protective of me. When a visiting dog rushed me at full speed, catching me behind the knees to flip me into the air, Nick was there. I landed on a hard slate patio and heard something snap—my femur. The dog was on top of me instantly, mauling me. A snarling Nick with his hackles up bit the dog, pushed the dog away, and then kept it at bay until help arrived. Nick was our guardian angel.

He helped my granddaughter get over her extreme fear of dogs. She would scream and run in the presence of any dog that approached her whether friendly or threatening, it didn't matter. When Katie was visiting, Nick would lie down at her feet, never intruding to nudge her or ask for attention. With that kind of endless patience, Nick taught my granddaughter to trust, and she conquered this colossal fear.

As we closed the memorial box with our notes tucked into a plastic bag to keep time and weather from destroying our tributes, we held hands and prayed at his final resting place in a sunny spot on my ranch. "We thank you for this guardian angel who saved lives, chased danger into retreat, and washed away fear."

I try to imagine what heaven is like for dogs. I know one exists because God wouldn't let these loyal creatures down with no reward. It must be a place with not just 10 acres, but a million acres, with an eternity of holes to dig and smells to sniff. If it turns out there really are pearly gates to heaven, I see Nick, waiting there for me, leash in his mouth, looking forward to another long walk.

Addie

She was a beautiful and sweet black-and-white cat. She had the longest hair of any cat I had ever seen so I had the groomer shave her body for the sweltering heat of July and August in California. She looked like a miniature lion, and I guess that's why the groomer called it the lion cut. There was a ruff of fur around her face and neck and a little pom-pom at the end of her trail. It made us all laugh to see Addie looking so adorable. We laughed again when she would stalk the wild turkeys in our yard, slinking through the tall grass. Suddenly the turkeys sensed her presence and turned in her direction. Addie stood straight up and looked like she might have been saying to the turkeys, "Wait. What?! Not me. I'm not doing anything." The turkeys would go on about their business. Addie would crouch down and stalk them again and the whole funny scene would replay several times until they all got bored with the game and went their separate ways.

We had taken her into our family at age two when her people were moving to Europe and had to rehome all their pets. My son, Evan, picked her out because she was the friendliest. She was used to living in the country with acreage to explore and tiny critters to hunt. At our place, she was definitely an outside kitty except when the weather was bad, and I would bring her inside.

Years went by before we had an unexpected crisis. A visiting dog had run at me from behind and flipped me up into the air. I landed on the hard slate patio and heard a crack. It was my femur snapping in two. Our hero dog Nick came to my rescue when the visiting dog began to maul me as I lay on the ground unable to move. Nick drove the dog away from me and kept him at bay until help arrived. I had emergency surgery to repair the break with metal rods and went home from the hospital in a couple of days to recover at home. I used crutches to get around a bit, but I heeded the advice to just take it easy but *easy* is not what I was used to, busy was more my style. So, I thought at least I could get some things done around our home that had been put off. The front windshield of my car had a crack in it that I had ignored for too long. I called a mobile repair business that would send someone out to replace the windshield.

I was startled when he showed up at my house. The man was a giant! He must have been at least seven feet tall and big too. I hobbled out to the car, Nick following me, to show the repair man the windshield. He started asking me weird questions. "How much pain do you have?" "Is it the worst pain you've had in your life?" "What would your dog do if someone threatened you?"

Yikes, I thought, *this man is strange.*

I didn't have time to ponder this odd questioning when a girlfriend showed up at my house with a basket of goodies for me to enjoy during my recovery. I invited her inside. Meanwhile, the giant began working on the car windshield out in the driveway.

My friend had barely sat down when Addie, our cat, came to the front door meowing again and again. I opened the door for her, and she rushed past me to the back door. I was puzzled but opened the door and she went out. Addie came around to the front door again meowing even louder than before. Again, I opened the door, and she ran past me to the back door wanting out. She repeated this odd behavior several more times. I told my friend this was not like Addie at all. I couldn't figure out what she was trying to tell me.

Then the giant came to the front door. When I opened it, Addie streaked by him. Every hair on her body was standing straight up in the air. Now I knew what she was trying to tell me. She was showing me that she was terrified of this man. She was telling me I was in danger. The giant saw my friend with me in the living room. He said he had forgotten a tool back at the shop and would need to come back the next day to finish the repair.

I thought this man meant to harm me. I don't know why. I got the feeling something terrible had happened to him as a child that made him confused about love and pain. Or maybe it was something else that motivated him to want to cause pain. Addie had confirmed to me and my girlfriend that this man could be violent. My friend stayed for a while after he left to be sure he didn't come back. Addie returned to her normal behavior snuggling in her cat bed on the patio.

When my husband got home, I told him what had happened and about Addie's behavior and my fear. He told me he thought nothing of it. I knew that Addie had told me something very important, something that helped me avoid a horrific experience. I told my husband I would not be at the house when the repairman returned the next day. I told him he would have to supervise and pay for the repair.

So that next day, I drove away in my husband's car with Nick by my side in the front seat. I passed the giant on the road and a chill went through me. I drove to a nearby church and sprinkled holy water from the vessel at the entrance on me and on Nick. I said a prayer of thanks to God for sending us Addie to watch over us. Anyone who says animals are dumb because they don't have language just hasn't learned their language. Addie was one sweet and smart cat.

Bella

In the horse world, a "heart" horse is that one you've bonded with more than any other, the equivalent of your human soulmate. That's what Bella was to me—my heart horse. I've been one of those horse-crazy gals since I was seven years old. I got my start riding my neighbor's show ponies when their only child grew too big to ride them. Many years and many riding lessons later I got my first horse. There have been a lot of horses since then and I have loved them all.

Bella was for sale because her owners walked away from an expensive board bill. They didn't have the money to pay Bella's bills, so they forfeited the horse. She was advertised as a dressage horse that might have the talent to become a hunter/jumper. She was a beautiful black Trakehner cross. That's a warm-blood breed of horse known for sturdy bones and a calm temperament. After years of challenges with a hot-blooded thoroughbred, I was ready for a calm horse. I wanted an uncomplicated jumper too. I went to where she was stabled to try her out. A teenager rode her first so I could see her way of going. Bella was lovely to watch with her big strides and natural collection. Then it was my turn to try her out. I was a little nervous since I didn't know her well and wasn't sure what to expect. There were some jumps in the arena, and she had been so nice for me at the walk, trot, and canter I decided I would see what she could do over fences. I fell in love with her over the first fence. I had just pointed her at the jump and sat on her back like a sack of sand. She completely ignored my lack of direction and took the jump without any help from me. I thought maybe that was just a fluke, so I tried her over another couple of small jumps. She was the same. I was sold.

At home, in my own arena Bella showed me she didn't want any direction from me. If I used a little more leg or hand to guide her, she balked. She didn't do anything naughty; she just didn't want to hear anything I had to say. Little by little I taught her she could trust me. She began to accept some guidance from me. This whole process took about a year but by the end of that time Bella and I were best friends. She still liked doing things her way but in the show ring over jumps that worked for us both. We entered the start gate for a round of jumps and all I had to do was gently guide her to the correct fence and she jumped it with pure grace.

She was trustworthy on trail rides too. Even when a mountain biker came whirling around a blind curve at high speed behind us Bella was steady. Another time her bridle broke, and I had to ride her with just a halter. She was every bit as responsive to me and calm as could be in a situation where another horse might freak out. We trusted each other. That trust is pure gold in the equestrian world.

For a few years, my husband and I trailered the horses

to Canada for the summers. He was a Canadian citizen and could only spend 6 months of any year outside Canada. As a U.S. citizen, I was only allowed to be in Canada for 6 months. So, we split our time between British Columbia and California. Bella and her pasture mate CeCe made the long trip back and forth without a complication or complaint. Bill turned out to be an excellent horseman and usually rode Bella since she was a full-sized horse and CeCe was a pony. We had a house in a nice community on Lake Okanagan in the southeastern part of British Columbia. We stabled the horses at a ranch nearby and could ride in a covered arena in any weather or out on miles of trails overlooking the lake.

There was trouble ahead. During our last stay in Canada Bella got sick. The ranch manager called us at home and said we should come take a look at her. When we got to the barn it was obvious Bella was colicking. She was biting at her sides and rolling to try and relieve the pain. Colic is a nasty condition for horses. To say it's a stomachache is to ignore the often-life-threatening nature of this gut disorder. Sometimes the colic involves a blockage, and the horse is unable to pass manure. Other times it can be caused by a twisted intestine but in either case colic is serious. Sometimes it can resolve on its own, or conservative treatment with fluids, and pain medication but other times surgery may be necessary to save the horse's life.

We called the vet to come out and evaluate Bella's condition. He confirmed it was colic and asked if we were open to a surgical approach. Many horses don't survive colic surgery and it is very expensive—often more than $10,000. Bella was considered a senior horse now at 21 years of age. I didn't want to put her through the risk of surgery, so I said no. The vet would try the conservative medical approach with fluids and pain meds. Bella seemed to respond well. She was passing some manure, eating almost normally, and drinking water. The vet said he had done all he could do for the time being. He was leaving on a trip the next day and would not be available to come back out. We crossed our fingers.

The next morning the phone rang early at our place. It was the ranch manager. He told us Bella had taken a turn for the worse. He told us to come right away. When we arrived, we could see Bella was in agony. She was pacing her paddock, rolling and biting at her flanks. She was much worse than before. All the other horses in the row of paddocks were calmly eating their morning hay. Even Bella's friend CeCe took no notice of Bella's suffering.

Bill and I watched in agony as Bella threw herself against the metal pipe panels because of the pain she could not escape. She hit her head hard and stumbled to stay on her feet. Again, the other horses were not at all alarmed by Bella's behavior or the noise she made when she crashed into the metal panels. By now I was beside myself with my own emotional pain. I realized we were watching her final moments. We had called other vets to come out so at least we could put her down and end her pain. No vets were available. I was going to lose my heart horse.

Bill and I were standing at the far end of her long paddock. At the other end stood a defeated Bella, head hung low, out of the fight, resolved she could not go on much longer.

Then suddenly she raised her head and turned to look past us. There was only the blank wall of the big barn behind us, but she was looking in that direction. Her ears were up and forward indicating she was seeing something. There was nothing we could see but she saw something. Now she turned toward whatever it was and began to trot, lifting her legs high in a beautiful dressage motion I didn't know she could do—passage. Bill and I thought she was going to go right through us and through the fencing. I shouted to her, "Bella, I have to let you go now. Please lie down!"

And she did. She collapsed and took her last breath. I was heartbroken. Though I was sobbing, I began to understand that what Bella had seen must have been heaven. I imagine she saw horses waiting for her on the other side of the rainbow bridge. They beckoned and she followed. That is my comfort now. Heaven is for all God's beings. I miss Bella so much, but I know I will be seeing her again and I will reach out and touch her soft nose and she will nuzzle my cheek.

CHAPTER 9

Deepening Through Love

LOVE IS the great healer and according to *A Course in Miracles*, it is the only thing that is real. So why did I think I had the answer to the rest of my life when I thought I will never love again? That's the answer!? Why on earth or in heaven would God say to us, "Just never love again. You'll be fine."

I had just come through a firestorm of deep spiritual growth in my life. I felt alive with love for myself. There's no room for someone else. I am enough by myself. There was a reckoning ahead—a miracle that changed my mind.

What Would Love Look Like?

Happy and terrified. The happy part because I had finally found the courage to leave a long and troubled marriage to create a new path for myself. The terrifying part was imagining another love partnership in my future.

I didn't trust my ability to choose someone worthy of my trust. I had been wrong in the last marriage. My husband had been so deceitful.

Now in my new life, I vowed never to put myself in that position again. So, the answer to my future had to be... *never love again*. That would be safer. Plus, I had enough love with friends, family, and my precious animals. I didn't need the intimacy of a man and woman relationship... too scary.

After a few months of exhilarating freedom alone in my new home, I began to confront the conundrum I had created with my decision not to love again. Growing within me was a deepening knowledge that God is love. And if God created me, then I was made of love. How then could I turn my back on love? I was afraid, that's why. Could I ever overcome this fear? At many times during my life, I have gone to bed with a question only to wake up the next morning with the answer. I have always listened to the answer, and I have always been grateful for this connection to a higher power. I felt the *truth* of an answer when it seemed to come unexpectedly, as such a surprise I couldn't possibly have thought of it myself.

I had moved to my new mini ranch in July. Now, at the end of October, I sat on the edge of my bed with my dilemma. How could the answer to my future be never to love again if love was the most important aspect of the universe? I waded out just a little in this murky water — *OK, God, if I ever were to love again, what would love look like?* As I rested my head on my pillow, ready to sleep that night, I thought if I got any answer at all, it likely would be a list of qualities to look for in a love partner, things like kindness, generosity, compassion, and so on. Maybe a list would be helpful. I just didn't know.

I awoke the next morning with a name shouting in my brain. It was so loud within my mind it jolted me upright in the bed. *What? Really?* Then that name again and again. I knew this name because I had thought about him over time. **Bill Lanterman!** I had expected a list in answer to my question about what love would look like. How could the answer be Bill Lanterman? I promised myself and God I would explore this big surprise.

What I knew, without doubt, was that Bill Lanterman had been my best friend in the world from third grade to my sophomore year in high school. We were together in school, always in the same class, every day. After school, and as young children, we played in the woods near our homes pretending to be warriors clearing the territory of dangerous predators.

One day in the woods, Bill surprised me with a plan for us to take a blood oath like the one we had seen between the Lone Ranger and his best friend Tonto on the popular 1950s kid's show. Bill had brought along one of his father's razors. We both took this promise seriously as we pressed our cut thumbs together and spoke our oath out loud — "We promise to be friends forever." Webster's defines the word "oath" as "a solemn appeal to God to witness to the truth of a statement or the sacredness of a promise." And that's how it felt at the time — like a truly sacred pledge.

Bill helped teach me about bravery. One day out in the woods as usual, Bill and another boy, decided to surprise me. They jumped off the top of a cliff. I thought they were going to die. Instead, they landed on a hidden ledge not far from the top and started laughing. Bill encouraged me from below, "Come on, Sue. This isn't what you think. You can do it!" I trusted Bill and guess I wanted them to see I was just as brave as they were. Even though I was scared, I jumped.

They knew something I didn't know. There was a cave under that cliff that couldn't be seen from the top. When I landed on the ledge beside them, they spun me around. There was the cave! What a treasure to share this secret. Jumping off a cliff was a lesson in courage and trust I carried with me all my life.

As children, we spent many hours outside together. At our homes, after coming in for dinner, we called each other on the telephone and talked for hours. We were inseparable. Our parents yelled at us to get off the phone, but we had so much to talk about I began taking babysitting jobs so I could call Bill after I put the children to bed. There was never a romance between us but rather a deep friendship built on trust and acceptance. Our talks were simple, usually conversations about school, but more importantly we allowed each other to talk about ourselves as people and how each of us felt about the world, our fears, and hopes and dreams. Neither of us would necessarily have an answer to our questions. And we never judged the feelings we expressed.

Once in high school, Bill asked me out on a double date with another couple. In the back seat of the car, on the way to a movie, Bill put his arm around me. It surprised me and made me worry Bill wanted to move this friendship in a new yet unexplored direction. During the movie, he put his arm around me again. I know I stiffened against this gesture and Bill got the message. I did not want romance — wouldn't that change the wonderful friendship we had together for so many years? At that stage of our lives, Bill and I didn't know much about romance, and we were not going to learn more about it then with each other. At the end of our sophomore year in high school, Bill's parents moved the family to Boulder, Colorado. I was sad to see him go, but there were no computers, email, or smartphones back then. We each let one another go. He was the gold standard of friendship. I thought I could find another best friend of that quality. Perhaps a romance that led to marriage would provide a partner with that same closeness.

Some 47 years later, with two marriages behind me, I was being challenged to reconsider what love really meant. Perhaps it was not about romance. Romance had morphed into troubled marriages. Maybe true love was about something else?

A divine power had told me that, quite literally, love looked like Bill Lanterman, the best friend I had ever had in all those years. I never found that level of trust and acceptance with anyone else. Could I find Bill now? The world had changed a lot in those decades we had been apart. I was aware that Facebook on the Internet had enabled people to find friends from the past. But what door was I opening if I found Bill? What if he didn't even remember me? Maybe I had fantasized our friendship into something more than it had really been? What if he turned out to be a drug addict or a compulsive gambler? Where had life taken him?

I gathered my courage and logged onto Facebook. My pulse was racing, and my anxiety level was rising. I put his name into the search box and clicked on it. To my surprise, at least a dozen Bill Lantermans turned up. I didn't recognize any of them. What if he's not on Facebook? What if I contact one of these Bill Lantermans, and it turns out he's not my Bill Lanterman but an axe murderer? OMG! What have I gotten myself into? One of the twelve mentioned in his brief profile that he had gone to high school in Boulder, Colorado. I barely remembered that Bill's family had moved to Boulder. Could this be my Bill? From his picture, I knew he was handsome but my memory of him at age 16 did not match this current photo. Boulder was my only clue. Was I brave enough to contact this man who might be a complete stranger? I had never looked up old friends before, never even went to one of my high school reunions. I sat there in front of my computer for what seemed like an hour. Should I send a message? Should I leave this search alone? In the end, I decided to trust that whatever door this opened would lead to greater wisdom.

"I am looking for an old friend and wonder if you ever lived in another state and went to a different high school?"

That's the Facebook message I sent to the man who wrote that he went to Boulder High School. *What a long shot! What have I done?*

I was so nervous the rest of the day, checking now and then for a return message. It was there in the morning when I awoke.

Bill had written back on Facebook, "Yes, I did live in another state, and went to another high school. Sue Pearson!! You mean my best friend who just happened to be a girl?"

I was ecstatic. I had indeed found my Bill, and he remembered the past just as I did — best friends! We traded Facebook posts, used email for longer notes, and decided to phone each other. By now, I had learned that Bill was married, had two grown sons, and lived in Nova Scotia. I wasn't even sure where Nova Scotia was but learned it was an east-coast Province of Canada. So very far away from where I lived in California, but Bill and I could write and phone. We soon learned that the friendship was still there and, repeating history, we talked and talked and talked. We reminisced about so many things we had done together as children: learning to dance, pairs roller skating, portraying the king and queen in a 4th-grade French play, joining Bill's baseball team as the only girl player, getting into mischief with snowballs and nearby railroad cars, watching the movie Psycho together and being scared of showers for the rest of our lives, riding the roller coaster at Glen Echo amusement park.

And then there was the game called Spin the Bottle. That was a big moment for both of us in this experience, and now, so many years later, we laughed about it and cherished it even more. We had gathered at a friend's house for a party. We were young enough that our parents had to drive us there. About a dozen of us partied in the basement recreation room. We had refreshments, played music, and danced to Johnny Mathis and then we got a little daring. Spin the Bottle was a kissing game. Most of us had never kissed or been kissed before so, this game was a little scary and very exciting.

With all the girls forming a circle we watched as a boy, Kurt, who was a foreign exchange student from Germany, took the empty Coca-Cola bottle and put it on the floor in the center. He sent the bottle into a spin and when it stopped it pointed to the girl who was to be kissed. Well, the more sophisticated Kurt swaggered over to the girl, put his arms around her, leaned her backward, and planted a very long kiss on her lips. The rest of us were shocked. This was a real kiss, the romantic kind we had only ever seen in the movies. Bill remembered feeling so nervous when the boys were on the circle and the girls had their turn to spin the bottle. I was nervous too. When it was my turn to be in the middle of the circle, I prayed I would not have to kiss the German boy. I'm sure I held my breath while the bottle spun and when it stopped it pointed right at Bill. I remember feeling such relief. *No problem giving my best friend a little kiss.* Bill was still worrying about a romantic kiss on the lips so when I leaned in with just the lightest and briefest kiss on his lips, and both of our eyes wide open, I think he was relieved too. Fifty some years later, he told me he never forgot that moment because it was his first kiss.

How sweet it is in these present moments to remember the milestones in our relationship.

As we spoke by phone and reminisced in emails, we started to share our experiences as adults, just as we had as children. I felt that I wanted to fully disclose all my most personal details. I told him about going back to college to get a degree after I had dropped out in my early twenties. He had done the very same thing but continued with school earning a PhD from Cornell University. He had two grown sons who both lived in Vancouver. In California, I had a grown daughter, a son, and three stepsons from a second marriage. I told him about my long years as a broadcast journalist moving into many different jobs within one television market, Sacramento, CA. I shared with him my health crisis during production of a documentary on strokes. I had a brain aneurysm repaired in an emergency procedure, which placed platinum coils into the bulging blood vessel behind my right eye. I had an other-worldly experience as I lay on the operating room table, fully conscious. I felt a peace come over me that transcended words but left a distinct message that I would be OK if I lived through this crisis or OK if I died. I felt very comforted by this. I could also hear the voices of my friends in another room down the hall expressing their concern for me.

I was hesitant to tell Bill about my other huge mystical experience of being present as my deceased mother helped my father transition to heaven. Some people are just not open to there being more to life than what our earthly senses tell us. I hinted to Bill that I had experienced a transformational moment when my beloved father was dying. He said he wanted me to tell him about it. Just as when we were children, he had not been judgmental about anything I had told him so far. I decided to open up about my deepest spiritual moment. Bill listened with great interest as I told him of seeing my mother in divine light lift my father up from his hospital bed and take him in her arms. I told him all I learned in those moments of God, love, forgiveness, eternal life, faith, and trust. He was awed by the story and thanked me for sharing it with him.

Bill then brought up the ideas of spirituality he had explored. He talked about Eastern mystics, Christian mystics, and various authors that had inspired him. He also shared that he had become quite interested in *A Course in Miracles*, which he felt embraced his deepest spiritual longings in a way that was free of the religious dogma that we had both explored, but also oriented to forgiveness in a way that had never been explained to him before. I became very interested by his excitement and attraction to this new path. I had hesitated to speak to him about my spiritual experiences because I was afraid that, in this new relationship, I might put him off. How wrong I was. We were still on the same wavelength.

Bill suggested I might like the book that had become so important to his own spiritual growth. I had heard of *A Course in Miracles* but had never read it. Now I was curious since it had been so meaningful to Bill. I found the book at a local bookstore and dove into it that same night. As I read the text, I found myself facing the same truths I had discovered in my mystical experiences. Every word in the book resonated as truth. What a huge comfort to feel at home in this book, scribed by a human being but said to be the words of Jesus Christ.

I let Bill know how excited I was to be introduced to this book. Some of it seemed a bit over my head so, I thought it might be a good idea to join a study group in my area. I found one hosted by Mary, a lovely, welcoming woman in El Dorado Hills just a 20-minute drive away. Most of the six to ten people who attended this weekly daytime gathering had been in this group for fifteen years. They were all experienced ACIM students. I was immediately struck by how patient they were with my inexperience. Within a few months, I felt deeply connected to these people. Meeting every week became a top priority in my life. There is something so powerful in the coming together of like-minded people.

I have not questioned whether my question: What would love look like? And the answer: Bill Lanterman, was divinely guided. But I was amazed at what ACIM had to say about questions and answers.

"In the holy instant you can bring the question to the answer, and receive the answer that was made for you."
(CE) T-27.V.7:7

"Bill Lanterman" was indeed the answer that was made for me. But now, in this reconnected friendship, I was not sure where the journey would lead. Perhaps this was an opportunity to understand more about true love, experience it from afar, and look for someone else closer with the same potential for deep connection. I had a level of trust with Bill that I doubted I could develop with someone else. I was willing to consider, though, that this was the lesson in our coming back together across the miles. At one point, Bill let me know he had been unhappy in his marriage. He didn't think either he or his wife were capable of the degree of change he felt would be necessary to heal the relationship. I told him I thought it was possible to transform within a relationship and I encouraged him to seek marriage counseling. This was a window into the quality of love I felt for Bill. On the one hand, I would have been thrilled to have him be with me but on the other, if he could be happy in his marriage I wanted that for him. Now it sunk in that the friendship I experienced with Bill those many years ago and today was indeed unconditional love. The moment we shared speaking our blood oath together had been a holy instant. How rare to love someone and yet be ready to let them go. Bill's happiness was his right. I wasn't sure how or if he could claim it.

Some years later, trusting in the connection we had as

children, now renewed in our later years, we made the mutual decision to be together. Bill's wife was very unhappy about the ending of their marriage. I am sure coming apart is difficult for most couples. Later, Bill saw his marriage relationship in a metaphor from *A Course in Miracles*. It spoke to him and brought clarity.

> "A desert is a desert is a desert. You can do anything you want in it, but you cannot change it from what it is. It still lacks water, which is why it is a desert. The thing to do with a desert is to leave." (CE) T-I.43.12:2-5

So, Bill and I came together for the second time in our lives. After several years of long-distance contact with one another, we were finally face-to-face. I melted into his arms, and we danced to Etta James' "At Last" on a patio at sunset overlooking majestic mountains. When the song ended, Bill looked at me and said, "You are not going to believe this, but as I look at your face, I see my own." At that very moment, I looked at his face and saw me. Oneness — that's what this relationship was showing us. We were together as one and shared our second holy instant.

> "One instant spent together restores the universe to both of you." (CE) T-22.VII.6

Three years later, we got married in the coastal town of Tofino overlooking Long Beach on Vancouver Island. The wedding was magical for us. We dressed up, looking quite handsome and sophisticated. We reveled in the beauty of the ocean-front setting and spoke of what our love meant to each of us. We told the marriage commissioner and our two witnesses our love story and everyone cried from the sweetness of the present moment and how long it had taken us to get there.

For a while, we divided our time between Canada and the US but then decided to consolidate and simplify, living year-round at our home in California. Just this morning, Bill found me at the computer. He had tears in his eyes as he handed me a book.

"Look at this." He smiled through his tears. He was in the process of cleaning out our garage and sorting through so many of his belongings. He had reached into a box and found a book he hadn't opened in fifty years and pulled out our high school yearbook from 1963.

"Turn to the second page," he said with a catch in his voice.

My mouth dropped open when I saw the inscription. It was from me when I was sixteen years old and saying goodbye to my best friend, Bill, who was moving to Colorado. It read:

"To my sweetest honey!

First, I want to thank you for supplying my lunch for the last year. Don't forget those card games and wild discussions we used to have. By the way, when do I get my engagement ring? I've been waiting for years. Oh yes, and don't forget the beach with Dick, me, Sherry, and Kathy...

Save a place for me in Colorado. I'm going to miss you so much.

Your True Love

Sue"

It turns out we saved a place in our hearts that transcended time and space. I had wondered whether Bill would claim his happiness, which is everyone's right. But he did. And I did too. Is it all that we hoped it would be? Yes, and so much more.

It never fails to fill me with humility and grace that when I glance at my Bill all these years later, I see love because I understand Bill Lanterman **is** what love looks like.

"From your holy relationship, truth proclaims the truth and love looks on itself." (CE) T-19.IV.B.9:4

CHAPTER 10

Deepening... The Journey Continues

WITH EVERY experience since I followed my father part way to heaven, my spiritual awareness has deepened. I have learned about holy encounters and am now alert to those opportunities with anyone to see their holiness. I have learned that divine guidance is always available to us if we can choose to put our own ego-based decision-making aside. I have begun to understand how my negative thoughts either consciously or subconsciously affect my health. I am getting better at putting my judgments about others aside. I have been shown a glimpse beyond the thin veil that seems to separate us from God. I have come face to face with true unconditional love. I can figure out when my ego is trying to take over by whatever seems to disturb my peace.

I am not an enlightened master. I am simply awakening a little bit at a time. Even though I understand miraculous forgiveness, that doesn't mean I extend it in every situation, though I try to if judgment and condemnation come into my mind. Forgiveness has mostly been a process for me, but I get there quicker than I ever did before.

Am I perfect because of all these amazing experiences I have had? No. I have made mistakes along the way and continue to make them. I am so much more adept at letting the past go, releasing guilt, and loving myself. I have more peace in my life.

William Peters of the Shared Crossings Project says this kind of deepening happens to many who experience SDE's. "Does the NDE and or SDE open a gateway kind of mystical, spiritual type capacity, and the answer to that is yes. We have a question that is very open-ended about that with our SDE experiencers, and I know it's the same in NDE's as well because I've looked over that research from our colleagues. The people will say that it was that experience that opened up some psychic abilities, some intuitive ability, and even mediumship. Some mediums, not all, but some will attribute their NDE or SDE and end-of-life experiences to opening up this capacity to connect across the veil."

During an ACIM Forgiveness Challenge offered by the Circle of Atonement, I was asked to look at all the people in my life and see the spark of beauty in them—even people I had thought of as enemies and, of course, those I considered friends. And yes, I could see a spark of beauty in them all. I have come to realize this spark of beauty is the portal to behold the holiness of each brother and sister. I realize this and see my own holiness. To me this is the most important part of my journey. If I can see the spark of beauty and thus behold the holiness in everyone then I can forgive everyone anything including myself.

How do you see that spark of beauty? Let me give you an

example from my own life. My oldest child, Christine, is all grown up with a child of her own now. Since she was a little girl, I could see how she cherished her friends and learned how to keep them close. She has kept them all through many decades. That is one spark of beauty in my daughter!

My youngest child, Evan, is all grown up as well. I remember meeting him for lunch in San Francisco quite a few years ago. At the time he ran an after-school program for kids in middle school. When we stepped outside the restaurant we heard a chorus of shouts, "Evan! Oh Evan, Yo Evan! Hey man!" Evan turned and looked across the street where a group of youngsters had gathered on the street corner. He smiled. "Oh Mom, those are my kids. I have to go over and make an appearance."

"Of course you do, my love," I said. There is a spark of beauty in my son!

My oldest stepson seemed troubled during his childhood. I very much wanted to give him an experience of just having fun. So, I drove the two of us to a property in the country we owned. I had built a tree house there for the kids and put up a tire swing on a long rope. He and I had a picnic lunch in the tree house. Afterwards, we took turns on the tire swing going as high as we could in the air. He smiled and he laughed again and again. There is that spark of beauty.

The middle stepson had a moment after his dad and I split up of thinking it might be better to distance me from his life. I was heartbroken. I couldn't imagine my life without him, his wife, and their beautiful twin daughters. But I let it be. Then one day when I was driving into town to run errands, he called me on his cell phone. "I was wrong. I need you in my life. My family needs you too," he said. "I want to come out to your place and bring the twins."

"That's wonderful!" I said. "When would you like to come?"

Without a pause he said, "How about right now?" There is that spark of beauty!

And now to my youngest stepson. Here is an excerpt from a letter I wrote to him when he was in high school. "You learned that by adding more people to your life to love, you didn't divide the love—you multiplied it. If this path taught you how to be open, non-judging, forgiving, caring, generous, fun, and funny, curious, creative, energetic, positive, and giving, then you have learned that love has nurtured the best in you." There's that spark of beauty!

All my children are beautiful through and through but the sparks I see serve as reminders of their holiness. I have been able to see that spark of beauty in a former friend I had considered an enemy. I see that spark in a dear friend I have held close for more than forty years. That beauty resides in both of my former husbands.

Once you have seen that spark of beauty in so many, you begin to pull open the imaginary curtain and see more of who they really are—they are holy sons and daughters of God. Now you can forgive and receive forgiveness for yourself. I believe this is the path that leads back to God. He's always been there, but you and I forgot.

To my evolving way of thinking, forgiveness offers everything I want. *A Course in Miracles* has a lot to say about the importance of forgiveness. Here's a sample:

Forgiveness is the great need of this world, but that is because it is a world of illusions. (CE) W-46.1

It is your forgiveness that will bring the world of darkness to the light. (CE) W-62.1

The light of the world brings peace to every mind through my forgiveness. (CE) W-82.1

He will teach you to remember always that forgiveness is not your loss but your salvation. And that in complete forgiveness, in which you recognize at last that there is nothing to forgive you are absolved completely. (CE) T-15.VIII.5

There is a lovely prayer about forgiveness:

Father... Help us forgive, for we would be redeemed. Help us forgive, for we would be at peace. (CE) W-359.1

A Course in Miracles lights the way for me, but it is only one of many paths that can lead us to truth. Some traditional religions can offer pieces of the truth that help us in this journey. I have a friend who has studied *A Course in Miracles* for many years. She has also been a devoted Catholic for many years. One of her sisters told her she was a "cafeteria Catholic." My friend thought that was a lovely compliment. Her sister had meant it as a criticism. Another ACIM friend of mine is Jewish and has for many years treasured the wisdom she has found in both paths.

Here are some powerful thoughts from other spiritual traditions:

From Sufism — "My heart has been rent and joined again; my heart has been broken and made whole; my heart has been wounded and healed again; a thousand deaths my heart has died, and thanks be to love it lives again."

From Kabala and Ba'al Shem Tov — "When we are wronged by somebody and instead of harboring anger and hatred toward them, we forgive them, all of the negative energy we have created is washed away."

From Hawaiian spiritualism, Ho'oponopono, a practice of forgiving and healing — "I'm sorry, please forgive me, thank you, I love you."

Rumi — "The wound is the place where the light enters you."

From the Bhagavad Gita — "When we have the ability to forgive others, we have surrendered our ego because the need to forgive others for their wrongdoings gives us peace."

From the Bible, Luke 6.37 —"Forgive and you will be forgiven."

From Eckhart Tolle — "Forgiveness is to offer no resistance to life—to allow life to live through you."

I want to acknowledge that for some people forgiveness feels impossible. Someone's bad or even monstrous behavior has hurt them. I still believe miraculous forgiveness can happen. This doesn't mean there aren't consequences for hurtful behavior in this world. It doesn't mean the person who has suffered from this bad behavior has to stay and continue to be abused. There are gifts in miraculous forgiveness that are worth receiving for both the forgiver and the forgiven. These gifts include peace, joy, gratitude, and compassion all aspects of God's love. Who wouldn't choose to trade the suffering, the hatred, and the guilt for these gifts. Here's the cornerstone of forgiveness according to Lesson 46 in the ACIM workbook, "God is the love in which I forgive." During my dark night of the soul, I thought God might come to me with pity or empathy for my suffering, but He didn't. He brought His indescribable pure love to me and lifted me up. It was in God's love that I began to forgive myself for my inaccurate perceptions. It was in God's love I began to understand I could forgive my former husband his own mistakes. Forgiveness was the doorway to healing.

From the Manual for Teachers in ACIM:

> *Until forgiveness is complete, the world does have a purpose. It becomes the home in which forgiveness is born, and where it grows and becomes stronger and more all-embracing.* (CE) M-14.2

A Course in Miracles makes bold statements about the importance of forgiveness and the consequence of not forgiving:

> **Forgiveness is the key to happiness.** *Here is the answer to your search for peace. Here is the key to meaning in a world which seems to make no sense.*
> (CE) W-121. 1

And what is the cost of not forgiving?

> *The unforgiving mind is full of fear and offers love no room to be itself; no place where it can spread its wings in peace and soar above the turmoil of the world. The unforgiving mind is sad, without the hope of respite and release from pain.* (CE) W-121.2

As a newbie teacher of God, I am not here in these words to tell you what to do, or how to do it, or where to go. I do hope to inspire you to find your own path back to God and the truth of who you really are: God's Holy child.

ACIM and other spiritual disciplines teach that this world is an illusion we have landed upon in our minds. I have a sense of this from my journey part way to heaven with my father. When I returned to the room in my father's Florida condominium from my glimpse of heaven, I knew that heaven was real and this world, not so much.

Though I don't offer you a map for the journey, I do have a few tips. First, find a way to quiet your mind. Our endless chattering distracts us from hearing the voice for Jesus or Holy Spirit or God Himself. It is in the quietness that we can connect with their holiness and their wisdom. They are better guides than our separate selves. Learn how to get in that stillness so you can connect with the divine. One way to do that is to meditate or just sit quietly and try to empty your mind. Lovely, soothing music can help you in this. So can guided meditation.

Jack Kornfield is a spiritual teacher with a background in Buddhist principles. His guided meditations have helped many people reap the benefits of quieting the mind. He offers this sample: "Rest in loving awareness, relax into it. Notice the breath, feelings, thoughts rising and falling. You are the mindful loving awareness itself, the loving witness to it all, spacious and wise." There are hundreds of online mediation offerings. Many are free, some offer subscriptions. Meditation Oasis is one of my favorites. I encourage you to sample the many styles of meditation out there in the world and find one that sings to your heart.

During the Circle of Atonement's Forgiveness Challenge, I created my own guided meditation. I imagined I was on a very large stage in a beautiful theater. The audience in front of me was huge. There was not an empty seat. The stage performance had just ended. My husband Bill and I came out from stage left and stage right to meet in the center and hold hands. The audience began to applaud. Then we each invited all those people who had touched our lives, both friends and enemies to join us on stage. They came out one by one.

Oh, look! There is the boss who called me an uppity broad and fired me from a job I loved. *Oh!* And there is the con artist who promised to build a beautiful playhouse for my grand-children and took off with the money. The woman I had called a friend, who sued me, was there on stage too.

My friends came out one by one; then my family joined me. My baby sister, Nancy, walked on, my parents, my older sister, and when my autistic brother joined us, the audience thundered their applause and gave him a standing ovation. *Good job Jon!* Bill's people came out too. And when we were all there across the big stage, we looked at one another and smiled. Great performances, all. Now we joined hands and lifted our arms in the way actors do when the play is finished. Together we all bowed to the audience. They all stood and applauded our performances. What a fantastic play!

"Thank you for coming," I say to you all. Blessings from my heart to yours.

NOTE: Lilies are often referred to as a symbol of forgiveness — the sure path back to heaven and home with God. Here is the last line of the poem St. John of the Cross wrote in *The Dark Night of the Soul:* "And amid the lilies forgotten, Threw all my cares away." From *A Course in Miracles:*

Yet will one lily of forgiveness change the darkness into light; the altar to illusions to the shrine of Life Itself. (CE) W-330,5

About The Author

Sue Pearson has been a professional journalist for more than 45 years. She is currently editor of the Story Project — a collection of true spiritual stories from people who are students of *A Course in Miracles* (*circleofa.org/story-project*). Her shared death experience has been published on the highly regarded International Association for Near Death Studies (IANDS) and was selected as a narrated feature by IANDS Radio host Lee Witting. Her story "You Don't Have to Die to Get to Heaven" has also been archived by the Shared Crossings Project (*sharedcrossing.com*).

Over her many years of writing nonfiction, she has contributed to quite a few published anthologies: *Opening the Gifts of Christmas* (Andrews McMeel Publishing) *Horse Crazy* (Adams Media), *Raging Gracefully* (Adams Media), *The Healing Touch of Horses* (Adams Media ISBN 10:1-59337-624-3) and *Faith, Hope and Healing* co-authored by Dr. Bernie Siegel and Jennifer Sander (John Wiley & Sons). She has written articles for Horse and Rider Magazine and spiritual stories for Guideposts Magazine.

After graduating from California State University Long Beach with a BA in Journalism Sue began her career in broadcast news in Los Angeles serving as night news editor at KHJ Radio, and news anchor at both KNAC Radio in Long Beach and KPOL Radio in Hollywood. In television, Sue has worked as a news anchor, talk show host and medical reporter for the three major network affiliates in Sacramento.

At public television station KVIE in Sacramento, she spent more than a decade writing and producing nationally distributed public television documentaries and directing celebrity hosts including Larry Hagman, Bruce Dern, Val Kilmer and others.

Sue has earned multiple Emmy awards, winning Best Information Program for her documentary on stroke, titled "RX for Stroke Prevention," hosted by ABC Medical Editor Dr. Timothy Johnson.